IN
THE
IMAGE OF GOD

by

ARTHUR C. PIEPENBRINK

dp
DISTINCTIVE PUBLISHING CORP.

In The Image of God
By Arthur C. Piepenbrink
Copyright 1993 by Arthur C. Piepenbrink

Published by Distinctive Publishing Corp.
P.O. Box 17868
Plantation, Florida 33318-7868
Printed in the United States of America

ISBN: 0-942963-28-8
Library of Congress No.: 92-31645
Price: $9.95

Library of Congress Cataloging-in-Publication Data

Piepenbrink, Arthur C., 1922-
    In the image of God / by Arthur C. Piepenbrink.
        p.   cm.
    ISBN 0-942963-28-8 : $9.95
    1. Pantheism. 2. Image of God. 3. Conduct of life. I. Title.
    BL220.P54   1992
    191—dc20   92-31645
                                                            CIP

TABLE OF CONTENTS

i

INTRODUCTION

Opening doors to knowledge should be a warm and glowing experience, for knowledge is the keystone to a happier and more useful life. Yet there are barriers which keep us from knowing more; the most prominent of these are prejudice and vested interests.

Information such as you find in this book is not particularly new. It has been voiced before in the writings of the sages of cultures past and present, but there is a time in the process of natural *unfoldment* when things like this come together in a more focused and unified happening.

In this book you will learn about the pressure of vested interests which keep doors closed in any endeavor; you will learn that we must always be alert to the threat which these vested interests pose to our best interest. Eternal vigilance, it has been said, is the price of liberty, and in a democratic society this responsibility falls to every citizen.

Here, particular light will be thrown on a time-honored precept that we are created in the image of God. If there are persons who ever had doubts about whether or not they were "created" in the image of God, the substance of this text should put their doubts to rest. Not only will this book show that our creation could not be otherwise, but it will illustrate exactly what constitutes such imagery.

Though millions of persons subscribe to the idea that we are indeed images of God because it is "so written," there may be only a few who have no misgivings on the subject. As we view the frailties and shortcomings of our kind, we can hardly escape asking the question, "How can this be the image of God?"

We find it difficult to reconcile the frailties of human nature with the picture of God as it traditionally has been

1

portrayed. The picture generally has been one that depicted God as a father-figure, all-powerful, compassionate, loving, just, perfect in every way — watching over the affairs of earth and its inhabitants in a parental fashion. We are admonished to believe that nothing can happen on earth or elsewhere that is not the "will of God."

Thus when sorrows befall us, when our grief becomes unbearable, when our people and natural environment seem to be in league against us, we are comforted only by the admonition that "God works in mysterious ways his wonders to perform." Finally, we are instructed not to question God's ways or God's laws or God's anything.

How can we ever know God if we do not question? How can we follow God's way and God's law if they are forever relegated to the realm of *mysteries*? How can we ever mend our ways if we don't know what's wrong with the way we're going?

A great philosopher and statesman, Abraham Lincoln, had this to say on the matter: "If we could first know where we are, and whither we are tending, we could better judge what to do and how to do it."

Our purpose here will be to look more closely into the matters which daily confront us. We will present a picture of God which is believable and neither mysterious nor impenetrable. This book is meant to be a reliable guide in the affairs of your life, and it will help you to know where you are and where you are heading. You will be better able to judge what to do and how to do it. Our aim is to strengthen the moral fiber of society by digging deeply into the "words of the wise," and while it may seem that some cherished traditions are at risk, we want to assure you that when traditions serve a good purpose, they are never at risk.

We will be emphasizing again and again that the true image of God cannot be tarnished or altered by what we, or others may say. If traditions of God are sometimes woven into magical tales, we cannot discount the moral value of those traditions, just as we cannot discount the heart-warming tales we relate to our children — tales which almost invariably demonstrate the power of good over evil.

1

A UNIVERSAL BEING

The System

There has been an abundance of literature written on the subject of God. There is a continuing effort to define and redefine the Absolute. Many scholars of the subject today would suggest that God is in everything and is everywhere. This is tantamount to saying that God *is* everything. Could God be anything less?

If we conceive God to be everything, then God is another name for the universe, or BEING, the universal principle which constitutes all existence.

When we say that God is the ALL, then we can no longer separate him from anything. We cannot rightly say that this or that is not godly. We can say that it is right or wrong, uplifting or depressing, harmonious or inharmonious, but we cannot rightly say that it is ungodly. Because of our failings or misadventures, we always considered ourselves inferior to some greater force or power which escaped misadventure — a force or power like ourselves, but perfect in every respect. It commanded us, since we were no match for its prowess in such forces

3

as that of the sun, the winds or the rains. Natural forces were the first gods; they were powerful beings who were depicted as superhuman personages. As people conceived of growing hierarchies of gods, they did not change this basic picture of a superhuman personage. Even when people finally conceived of one supreme god over all other things, the god was still a superhuman entity, directing and commanding the elements of existence even as we commanded the elements of our environment, although in a somewhat more majestic and more enormous way.

Many scholars on the subject are inclined to be pantheists. To the pantheists, the ideals once ascribed to a supernatural being or personal god are transferred to the ideals of our own inner nature, to the *nature/being* of which we are part. We don't have to seek to be *one* with God, for we are already *one* with God, with the universe. We need rather to seek to be in harmony with this great principle, that is, with ourselves. We seek not only to know what God is, but rather to know all that we can about our own nature, which we equate with God.

A pantheistic concept of God greatly alters a person's philosophical and mystical outlook on life. Primary among these are the concepts of good and evil. Since in this belief all things are *one*, then evil isn't as evil as once thought; or the universal principle actually abides evil. The presence of evil, or negative aspects, is readily apparent in life, but we rarely have reconciled ourselves to seeing this as a god-phenomenon. We always chose to make our personal deity the ultimate in goodness. Thus deity was always favored with positive qualities, whereas it really is responsible for everything which happens to us, by the pantheist's definition. As a consequence we assigned all that affected us badly to an opposing deity, another superhuman force or being which was always the cause for our failures, for our lack of faith, for our misfortune and wrongdoing. At first there were many of these bad gods, too, but eventually they were all subordinated to one super bad god, such as Satan or Lucifer.

The pantheist's view may seem to dethrone the God

of our basic traditions, but in reality it enlarges the area and depths of God's kingdom, giving substance to the true greatness of our magnificent universe. It opens the doors to reason and scientific inquiry which too often have been seen as "partners of the devil." Rather than being evil, however, reason and scientific inquiry only seek to bring the unknown into the realm of the known. Their findings aren't always palatable to the "establishment," but they are the elements of God's kingdom which have brought to our doorstep the many wondrous possibilities for improving the lot of lifeforms here on earth.

We need to see in this great God-principle a reason for all that we are, for the highs of our lives, for those hours and days of love that fill our hearts with gladness and hope; just as surely, we need to see in it a reason for the lows of our lives and for the sense of loss and disappointment we often suffer.

For this we need to employ our reason, to open doors of knowledge which have previously been closed to us. The age of reason and scientific inquiry has been upon us for only a short period of time, but it is our present and our future; once the doors are open, there's no going back. You can only gain in knowledge. Once you *know*, there is nothing which can take that knowledge from you. You cannot "un-know" anything.

In this text, we are opening more doors so that you can see and feel more closely the awesome presence of God, especially as it applies to the development of a greater understanding of its positive, soul-satisfying qualities.

Within this text, the viewpoint is taken that God, Nature, Universe, and Being are all the same thing. Therefore, as a choice of terms that will better serve a universal understanding, we shall usually use the term BEING, primarily because it is without gender and personality. *Universe* and *Nature* are not suitable, for they often apply to only parts of the whole, as in "the many island universes," or "the natural and the unnatural."

BEING is preeminently a "system," an orderly arrangement of parts. It has parts, and it has order. For the purposes of this text, we are going to depart from some of the more traditional and popular ideas about BEING and posit a new set of guidelines in order to better understand the System as a simple, unified whole.

BEING is single in the sense that it is the only thing which exists. It is really difficult to imagine more than one BEING, first by our definition that BEING is all-inclusive, and second, by reasoning that there must ultimately be one super-unit of itself that contains in it everything else. There are always larger units into which we fit the elements of our existence. For example, a collection of cities or states makes up a country, a collection of countries makes up a continent, a collection of continents makes up a planet, a collection of planets makes up a solar system, and so on, until we reach the last unit which includes everything.

The size and limits of BEING elude us. Because BEING is everything, we say that it is unlimited — eternal in time and infinite in space — even though we cannot grasp the concepts of infinity and eternity. It is difficult for us to even imagine BEING *having* a beginning, for how could something come from nothing? This is not to say that our particular area of galaxies did not have a beginning, such as the "Big Bang." In the vastness and eternity of the system, however, that would simply be another stellar event, one of many such happenings in the infinity of space and the eternity of time.

Thus our starting point is not to concern ourselves with the how, when, where, or why of our origin, but merely to discover fully *what* we are. When we know that, we are in a position to set a course in life which will be in harmony with the natural order of things, thus pleasing and satisfying.

We should fully realize that all that anyone believes and holds to be true is merely opinion. That goes for the content of this work as well. A person can judge the usefulness or validity of this work only by comparing its contents with personal experience or personal reasoning. An opinion may be true, but we should never lose sight of the fact that it has no more basis for truth than the mind of the person through which it issues. Furthermore, opinions do not change the actual basis of things, only the way in which people perceive them. What is said here doesn't change the true state of BEING, but only the way in which we perceive it.

There are, in fact, only two things of which we can be absolutely sure, and those are: **we are** and **we know that we are**. As to *what* we are, that is a subject of never-ending research. What we hope to achieve here is to give you a basis for a discovery pattern all your own. We will touch only on some very fundamental concepts of BEING, concepts which are not new or original in this work, but concepts which are assembled in a new and different way, for these times, and for an awakening social consciousness.

A study of the nature of BEING can generally be divided into two sections: that which is *actual* and that which is *realized*. When we speak of *reality*, we are referring to the real world, the BEING which we realize, rather than the true state of BEING. **Reality is not a false concept of BEING, but it is an individual concept, colored and interpreted by the mind of the observer**. *Actuality* is the true state of BEING, that which gives rise to the realities in our consciousness. Of course, we deal exclusively with realities in our day-to-day activities, but it is nevertheless very important to understand the actualities behind them.

The actualities of BEING must almost by necessity be simple in structure, for it is difficult to conceive BEING as having a complex structure, since it is so orderly and stable.

A Trinity of Components

The actualities of BEING are not too difficult to discern if given just a few moments of thought. Look around you; notice that you can catalogue all the elements of your life into three basic components: 1) things all about you — objects outside and mental images inside — all things of which you can ever be aware. These we will call **substance**; 2) evidence of a **force** flowing through substance, bringing movement and animation to it; 3) that which gives life a sense of awareness and direction — this we will call **mind**.

As you observe the events of any day, you will always find these three elements, and only these three elements. Thus we can safely assume that these three elements are the *actuality* of our existence, or the basic components of BEING. Let us list and identify them here:

Substance

First, there are the things of our inner and outer surroundings, all of the *things* of which we are conscious. This is the *body universe*, including the seas, the land, the planets, the animal and plant forms, the products of our skills and our ideas — every-*thing*. These compose the **substance** of our existence. Anything of which we can be aware is a *thing*, part of **substance**.

Force

Second, there is an energy, or **force** which permeates the **substance** and gives it motion. We can readily observe that the System is not inert, that there is motion and activity everywhere. This **force** is electromagnetic in nature, and accounts for the behavior of all *things*, from orbiting satellites to the loves and hates of our relationships. It dictates the order of all behavior, as in these specific ways:

1. In its polarization into two poles, positive and negative, it creates attraction and repulsion between *things*, with like poles repelling and unlike poles attracting. *These poles are the "opposites" of our existence.*

2. Because of the System's motion, the polarities are in a state of flux, resulting in the altering or reversing of the attraction or repulsion quotient in any given relationship. What one may be attracted to now, one might be repelled from later, and *vice versa.*

3. In its tendency to follow the line of least resistance, it takes "the easy way out," a phenomenon which has countless ramifications. As it applies to human behavior it could, on the one hand, be an economy

of energy and time. On the other hand, it could be procrastinating and shirking of responsibilities.

4. It acts as a self-governing agent in maintaining the order of the System by virtue of these properties. Whereas the motion of the System tends to upset the balance of its parts, the mutual attraction of its polarities tends to bring them back into balance again, in a continuing see-saw, pulsating manner. The motion of the System, since the System already occupies all space, is not taking the System anywhere. Therefore, the motion is likely to be of a pulsating nature, beating in a constant, rhythmic fashion. Socrates pointed out that generation cannot be forever in a straight line. This is not difficult to see in the actions of the System's manifestations, from a simple heartbeat to the expansion and contraction of stellar phenomena.

Mind

Third, there is **mind**, an integral part of the System, in spite of the fact that it is often ignored in our study of nature, with focus remaining on **substance** and **force**. **Mind** is neither **substance** nor **force**, nor is it a product of these. It stands as a full, separate component of the whole, although there are schools of thought which declare that *all* is **mind**, or that *all* is *energy*. **Mind** accounts for consciousness, and is involved with the ego, or self; but it is neither a *thing* nor a **force**. There is only one **mind**, and all the appellations applied to it, such as *objective*, *subjective*, *the unconscious* and *the subconscious* are simply cataloguing the different ways in which **mind** manifests itself.

Mind accounts for two characteristics of the System: its ability to be aware of its existence and its ability to direct the activity of its parts within the limits of its inherent structure. (In our context we shall be using the terms *consciousness* and *awareness* synonymously.)

The System is not a creation of a previous, thought-out plan, and there is no reason for its being what it is. It simply *is*. It always has been and always will be. It cannot be other than what it is, and in that sense, it is limited. It has no consciousness of itself as a whole, as against something else which it could identify as separate from itself, and in that sense it is limited as well. It, like everything in it, is subject to the law of its order, and this law is, that for every action there is an opposite and equal reaction. This is Natural Law, simple, forthright, and unwavering.

It is to this law which we will refer many times in our later discussion on moral behavior. In our daily lives, Natural Law isn't always evident in the hurtful and criminal offenses which seem to go "unpunished," for although the law is absolute in its application, reactions are not always readily forthcoming. Reactions are often delayed for one reason or another, often by the stress-and-release factor wherein stresses build up to a point of explosive release in varying degrees. Examples of this are the build-up of gasses and molten rock inside a volcano, or the build-up of anxieties harbored by a person — the first being released by a volcanic eruption, the other by a temperamental or emotional outburst. It is thus important to be aware of the build-up of stresses in the people and things around us, so that we can take action to prevent their catastrophic release.

We are equating Nature's characteristics and behavior patterns with our own. The bottom line is that both are the same. The System's order is the order of all existence. The System is *it*. There is nothing else, and we are parts of it. We and Nature literally are *one*. If we study Nature and understand it well, we will also understand ourselves.

It is through its life forms that Nature gains consciousness of itself. Through life forms and their remarkable faculty to sense their own existence, Nature is conscious of itself; in the context of Natural Law, it can act upon itself with some notion of choice in the matter.

We can never repeat too often that the System is not some super entity apart from its manifestations, a super entity that somehow overlooks the whole world, making decisions to do this or that, enacting new laws from time to time, or nullifying old ones. There is no one running the System from the outside. All things proceed by its inherent law and order. There is no higher appeal than itself. We live with Nature as it is, and it is up to us to learn enough about it so that we can have a life in which we enjoy the peace of mind which balance and harmony bring.

We are now on a literary train in our quest for an answer to *what* is right, and *what* is wrong. Our destination is to know *what* we are, *why* we are as we are, and *how* to change any of the foregoing. First, there has to be a general understanding in the world regarding the System, as outlined in this text. Then there must be a general agreement that all people will do their part, not first waiting to see if someone else is doing it. One of our frequent excuses for not doing something is that we are waiting to see if other people are doing it. Conversely, we also admit that we behave in certain ways because everyone else is doing it.

There is no absolute right and wrong in the System as a whole. It cannot have the sensitivities in whole which it has in its parts. Again, we say that there is no Super Being apart from its manifestations which sees, feels, hears, or in any way is sensitive to its environment. Think for a moment, what it would be like if such a Super Being felt and sensed all that happens in Nature — the hot breath and exploding innards of a sun, the chilly cold of outer space, the collisions of stellar bodies. Ouch! Where would the right and wrong of those things be?

When flood waters inundate thousands of acres of land, killing millions of life forms, including people, we don't point a finger and say, "That was wrong!" When volcanoes erupt or hurricanes blow, doing as much damage as a flood, we don't fault the System. When there are those who escape catastrophe for one reason or another, we can't say that they were selected by the System to be spared; nor can we say, when harvests are bountiful and rainfall greens the land, that the System interceded and granted special favors to those involved.

These are neither right nor wrong acts. They are simply the outgrowths of the System's intrinsic nature.

It is only in the realities of life forms that these values come into play. Yet, even then, right and wrong are not cast in concrete, but are rather, relative values which we assign to the action-reaction chain of events. The System has its *law*, and everything proceeds from that law, without exception. The System is, if anything, *fair* in this regard. In it every event is a natural event. It could not be otherwise, since all things are a part of Nature. The System is perfect, in the sense that it is a complete entity, operating as a balanced whole, self-sustaining, self-disciplined, without any questions that it might veer from its course. Once understood, the System is predictable, following a course or action which echoes through eternity, without variation; on this we can bank.

However "perfect" it may be in its structure, we often find in our conscious experiences that not everything is as rosy as we'd like it to be. Why do we have to be susceptible to illness? Why do we have to grow old? Why do we have to go through a growing-up period? Why are we faced with a great dilemma of wanting to stay at rest and at the same time be pressed to change and adapt to the motion of the System? Why do we have a body which needs to be fed and watered, a body which creates waste which needs to be cast away? Why are we beset with feelings of jealousy, envy, anger, hate, and boredom? Why do plants and animals have to feed on each other to survive, with all the bloodshed and uprooting that this entails?

In short, *why* are we as we are?

The sooner we accept the premise that the events of Nature are not planned nor purposely ordained, the sooner we will seek to bring about a more responsible society. The study of Nature will be the first science of our schools, wherein **mind** will take its rightful place alongside **force** and **substance**. Then children will learn why they behave as they do just as readily as they learn why it rains, because there is only *one law* which covers all things. Why the students should be good will be as much a science as why it rains.

After this brief outline of the premises we are making, we shall proceed with a discussion of the operative aspects of the System. The System is made up of a single substance, the **substance** we mentioned earlier. This **substance** is in motion, activated by **force**. The motion is in the form of vibrations. These vibrations of the elementary **substance** are measured by their frequency of appearance, as in "number of vibrations per second," just as we measure their counterparts in the world of our senses. Light waves have a certain frequency. Sound waves have theirs, and electronic components have theirs. We do not know the range of frequencies in the elementary **substance**, because we can only be aware of those which affect our own sense apparatus or can be measured according to the sensitivity of our instruments. It very well could be that there are vibrations of **substance** with frequencies beyond those we perceive on our plane of existence. However, we will concern ourselves only with what we do perceive. Chances are that given the order of the System, its manifestations at any level correspond with each other.

What we have now, is one universal **substance** vibrating in a relatively large range of frequencies, with a particular spectrum we come to know as our *reality*. Even in the "particle" world of today's sciences, each atom has its specific vibratory rate, and thus we are already measuring basic particles in terms of nonparticle **substance**. At this moment, physicists are still looking for the *first particle* on which the material world is built. However, an electronic microscope has already shown that beyond particles there is just **substance**.

More important to us in this text is the part which consciousness plays in the make-up of the System. Consciousness is manifest only when the elements of the System reach a critical arrangement; then like a fire which flares at the stroke of a match, like a light bulb which illumines at the touch of a switch, like the forceful explosion of an atomic bomb when atoms mingle in the right proportion, like all *manifestations* of Nature, consciousness lights up our lives by the proper mix of **substance**, **force** and **mind**.

It is only in the consciousness process that the vibrations of **substance** take form, and each form is a vibratory configuration of **substance**. Configurations are a mix of various wave frequencies which combine to give us a particular reality.

While some sciences on the subject still search for particles which are basic to our realities, the wave configuration theory offers a broader explanation for the behavior of things than does the particle theory. The two theories are not far apart, however. In atomic physics, the "particles" of matter have their vibratory rate, and electromagnetism plays a large part in their structures. Both atoms and vibratory configurations are invisible to the naked eye and become visible or apparent to our senses only through the mechanism of our sensory apparatus. The wave configuration theory is not new, and was already postulated in some age-old writings.

Now we will analyze the sensory process in order to arrive at some insights into the nature of perception.

MECHANICS OF
PERCEPTION

Perception is the process of realizing the imagery inherent in the wave forms which are carried to the brain. It is important to realize at the outset that both the mechanism of perception and the things perceived are made up of the same *stuff*, or substance, of Nature. Both are vibratory configurations of Nature's basic **substance**, each with its specific rates of vibration. Perception occurs when a specific configuration of vibrations has developed in **substance**. At a critical point in this development, the **mind**-component of the System comes into play, and we are conscious! The point where this wave-mix occurs becomes a center of awareness, and vibrations flood into this center the way radio waves flood into the core of a radio receiving set. In the intricate and marvelous mechanism of a living organism, the waves take form and we experience the glories of Nature in all their beauty and depth.

How we perceive the waves of Nature which flood through our center of consciousness depends not only on the configuration of the waves themselves, but equally upon the configuration of the mechanism through which waves are perceived. Any aberration in the perceiving mechanism will distort the wave forms coming through, thus creating a different impression in the center point of consciousness than that which would have been created in another center of consciousness.

Without the mechanism in living organisms, there would be no awareness — no sounds, sights, feelings, tastes, odors, or thoughts. The waves from our environment which produce these phenomena would still be there, but they would not be making any conscious impression on us. We can draw a comparison to this by referring to common radio and television signals. At any given time, the waves which they produce are all about us. They abound in the substance around us. Still, they make no impression on us until we provide a receiving mechanism through which they take the forms which we know so well as sounds and pictures. And the same could be said for the other waves which titillate our sense mechanisms and take form as odor, taste, touch, or thought.

Note that *thought* is included as a normal sense experience. Thoughts are the result of imagery drawn from the information in our center of consciousness or appearing from some external source, either voluntarily or involuntarily.

Thought sources can be from our ideation, such as when we *think* of an object from the countless memory patterns we have stored in the brain — which come into focus on request or appear at random in our dreams and fantasies — or from thought patterns radiated from others.

It will be helpful here to review some basic biology and roughly sketch what happens in perception. We will then translate this process into a unified wave happening.

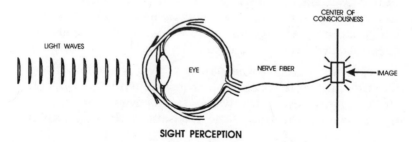

SIGHT PERCEPTION

When this very basic diagram is first studied, it seems to portray a very elementary concept. For example, light waves impact the eye; sound waves, the ear; touch waves, the skin. The sense organs then send a message to the central nervous system, and we say that we *see*, or we *hear*.

On further analysis, what is really happening when we say "we see," or "we hear"? It makes the phenomena appear to be *active* behavior on our part rather than *passive* behavior. Perception is a passive process, and it is something which goes on *within* our being, rather than *outside* our being. It is in the center of consciousness where the mix of vibrating **substance** takes form, and it is there that we are conscious of whatever imagery we perceive. There are no holes in our head through which we look out onto a world of matter or through which we project outward what is in our center of consciousness. The only thing on the outside is vibrating **substance**, first in the form of light waves or sound waves, then in the form of nerve impulses going from the eye or ear to the brain; it is there that the light goes on. We are *illuminated* with multidimensional objects, with the color and sound which accompanies them. *Perception is an inner event* which — through the intricacies of a lifeform's structure — gives us a *realization* of an external world of depth, shapes, and colors.

This is not to say that what we perceive is only an illusion and has no basis in fact. There is indeed a basis in fact for whatever we perceive. We cannot perceive anything that doesn't exist. **Substance** is the basis in fact. Its complex vibration patterns carry the potential of the imagery they generate.

One of the more common illustrations related to this phenomenon is the production of stereophonic sound through headsets such as those used in airplanes or home electronic equipment. If you have never listened to a "stereo" recording by way of earphones (headsets), it is an experience you should make an effort to have.

Then note: When playing a stereo musical selection, hold just one of the ear pieces to one ear. What do you hear? — a faint, more or less squeaky sound, hardly audible. You can do this to the other ear as well. Hold just one ear piece to the ear. Then place both ear pieces to your ears, and what do you experience? An almost unbelievable musical experience, rich and full, with great depth and volume, nothing at all like the little squeaks you first heard. This full, rich rendition happens in your *center of consciousness*, and it is there that the orchestration happens.

We refer again to two terms which are used in this discussion: *actuality* and *reality*. *Actuality* is the true state of existence. *Reality* is the way in which we are aware of it. Thus, an apple's true state (*actuality*) is a vibratory configuration of **substance**. Its realized state (*reality*) is a round, tasty ball of fruit, with color and dimension.

In the whole picture, the System is the single *actuality* of existence, and our time-space dimensional world is one way in which it is realized, or perceived, by us. The reality which we perceive is as much *actuality* as it is *reality*, for in essence the two are the same thing. There could be no *reality* unless there were an *actuality* behind it. We can draw a comparison here to the particle theory of matter, wherein a *realization* of the compound, water, would be in *actuality*, atoms of hydrogen and oxygen.

In either case, we could easily think that *reality* is just a figment of our imagination, and that none of our perceptions reflect the true state of Nature. However everything is a part of Nature. In our work-a-day world, we need to live by our perceptions which, being common to all of us as a species, provide us with an ordered environment with which we can deal.

In effect, our *reality* helps us to deal with *actuality* by giving *actuality* a form with which we can work — length, width, depth, time, space, color, taste, feeling, sight, hearing, and ideation. These are measurable units, and they give us a fullness of life.

Why then bother with a discussion of *actuality* at all? Why be concerned with it? As in every situation of our lives, when problems, questions, or stresses arise concerning the elements of our *reality*, it is essential to go back to the *source* in order to fully understand what is going on around us. Going back to a primary source gives us an answer to the ultimate *whys* of our existence. As we develop our presentation here on the *actuality* of our existence, you will be able to better understand its manifestations in *reality*.

In further developing this hypothesis, let's again look at our previous illustration, only now using a simple illustration of a single act of perception — "seeing an apple."

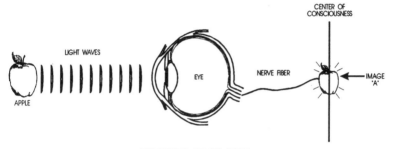

PERCEPTION OF AN APPLE

Our first awareness of an apple is at Point A. Light waves impact the eye mechanism. There they are converted to nerve waves, which travel along the optic nerve to the center of consciousness, A. It is *there* that we have an apple image, not out in front of us somewhere, but back there in the bowels of our brain structure. But do we "see" an apple there? Not at all. We *perceive* the image as an external *reality*. Through this marvel of our being, what is in effect an inner happening becomes a wondrous multidimensional world of shape and color external to ourselves.

The vibrations which impact our center of consciousness become our *reality* of the moment, and our realities change as we move about and interact with other **substance**. For the most part, our everyday realities are shared by all humans alike. The order of our existence depends on that. When **substance** vibrations give us the image of an apple, we can generally say that those same vibrations will give rise to the concept of an apple for other life forms as well.

When someone says we don't all "see" things the same way, the statement would be better stated, "We don't all describe our images the same way." Out of any hundred people who observe a given apple, we may hear different descriptions, but this is not because the image in their center of consciousness is any different, one from the other.

Different "sight" descriptions of an apple might run like this: it's a bright red, it's scarlet; it's a rich pink; it's burgundy; it's a deep, purplish red; it's red, on the pink side. "Taste" descriptions would also vary; for example: it has a sweet taste; it is rather bland; it seems a little mealy; it tastes more like a dull peach; it's as tart as a cherry.

There are times, however, when some persons actually "see" something differently than do their human counterparts. It is not because the **substance** vibrations are changing, but rather because the mechanism of perception has been affected in one way or another. At this point we will illustrate some of the several ways in which our perception of things is altered.

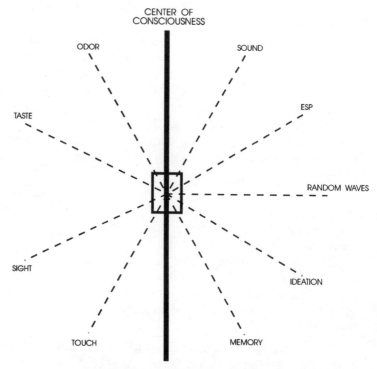

A BARRAGE OF SIGNALS

This illustration simply expands on the previous one, but it serves to show how very many things impact our consciousness and how difficult it can be for us to sort them out. Yet, we do. We take from this barrage of information only that which we want to use. We tune in to just those impressions which we wish to bring into immediate awareness. For example, as we walk down a busy street, we are selective in what we register in our consciousness. We remember certain sights and sounds, but for the most part, the countless other sights and sounds which came to our sense organs never made a significant impression. Our "tuning" mechanism is made up partly from our thoughts — with which we *decide* what we want to perceive or remember — and partly from the imprints already in place at birth. We see these imprints as instincts — automatic responses to given stimuli, things we do without thinking.

Instincts are not always reliable, for they do not arise from an unimpeachable source, as is sometimes thought, but rather from experiences of the species as carried in the genes. Thus, they may not apply in current situations. For example, in the far distant past, our species may have developed a reasonable fear of something, such as the fiery eruption of a volcano. This fear, carried forward as a fear of fire may be beneficial if it keeps us from getting burned; this fear may be a disadvantage if it keeps us from facing the challenge of fire and from utilizing its beneficial aspects. Nevertheless, when all else fails, it's not too bad a piece of advice "to go with your instincts."

Thoughts, as a process, act as a "tuning" mechanism or a switch, turning *on* or *off* many perceptions which we have. With thought we can decide what we want and what we don't want in our consciousness. Thought is a very powerful tool in ridding ourselves of *unwanted* perceptions. For any number of reasons, however, we aren't always ready to "let go" of *negative* perceptions. Thought is just as powerful in bringing into consciousness such *positive* perceptions as things we want to do or things we want to attain. Again, however, for any number of reasons, we aren't always ready to clear our consciousness of distractions and negative perceptions, something which is very necessary to experiencing the marvelous results of creative thinking.

We do not think often of our physical bodies as electrically operated mechanisms. The intricacies of every system within the body is powered by electricity. Sometimes we treat blood as the most vital element of our being, for we have found that without blood, we could not live. However, if we turned off the electricity in our systems, we would likewise die. Without electricity there would be no pumping of the heart, no flow of life-supporting blood, no flexing of muscle, no phenomenal exchange of data within the brain and neural pathways. Keeping this in mind, you will readily see the important part which the electrical system plays in our perception of things.

As in any electrical system, the proper functioning of such a system depends on the mechanism through which electrical power courses. Systems are often beset by short circuits — wherein wires cross in irregular fashion — or by injuries to and aberrations of one or more parts of the mechanism, all of which may interrupt the flow of **force**. Such interruptions will shut down parts of the system, and when this happens to vital parts, we can have everything from an itch to a major illness such as cancer, where cells are in disarray over a loss of direction.

Any difference in the structure of the **mechanics** of perception will in some way alter the imagery perceived by those mechanisms. If the lens of one's eye has a somewhat different curvature, it may cause the individual to perceive objects smaller or larger than the person next to him. Probably this, in itself, would never be discovered; if the person's eye slightly distorts an object, however, such distortion could be found out if the person is asked to draw what is perceived. Knowing this, we should not be too hasty in wronging persons regarding their observations, since they may be having a perception different than ours.

- Perception of things can be altered by variations in the structure of the mechanisms of the body.

- Perception can be altered by injuries or damage to the brain and neural pathways of the body.
- Perception can be altered simply by our own thinking, as when we fantasize.

Each of the above three conditions could give us an image of *actuality* different from that of our neighbor.

We might take space here to enlarge on the whole relationship of our *reality* to our perception mechanism. It can be a truly challenging mental exercise to contemplate the significance of what we are saying.

We cannot escape the fact that the tiniest particles of matter, the smallest increments of time (now measured in billionths of seconds) or the largest distances we can perceive for outlying galaxies are all measurements which are made in our center of consciousness, in a frame of reference dictated by the structure of our conscious processes. Thus we ask, "How far is far?" and, "How big is big?" — when the very size and distance of things are part of an illusionary *reality*.

Imagine, for a moment, that you are sitting in a theater, and a very tiny image on a piece of film becomes a grand expanse on the theater screen. If you brought the screen closer to the film, the sizes and distances would be greatly diminished. If you moved the screen (enlarged, of course) to a distance of 1000 yards, the image sizes and dimensions would fill your whole scope of vision and become a "living" world in front of you, as far as your eye could see. Computer enhancement of photos can bring other such demonstrations of the real and the actual.

Even the senses of touch, taste and smell can be introduced into such mechanisms, in order to truly present a "mechanical," total *reality*.

Reception and Transmission of Imagery

Many *things* can affect our perceptions. There is a collection of conditions which affect our *reality* on a day-to-day basis; in a standard dictionary they are all lumped under the definition of *intuition*, "direct knowledge without conscious attention, reasoning, concentration..." For the purpose of our discussion, intuition will mean only those perceptions, or flashes of knowledge, which come as a result of direct contact with the **absolute**, as we will explain later. Our breakdown then, of the principal conditions which can affect our *reality* is as follows: suggestion, hypnotism, habitual responses, random wave patterns, memory interference and intuitive flashes.

This general collection of conditions is also referred to as psychic perception or extra-sensory perception (ESP). While *psychic perception* is an apt term, *extra sensory perception* is not. ESP implies that impressions from these various sources impact the brain or center of consciousness without going through a transducer of some kind — such as a special sense organ in the head which receives wave information on that level and regulates what passes through and what does not, much as the organs of hearing or sight transduce sound and light into a frequency which evokes imagery in the brain.

Remembering that our *reality* is an inner experience, formed in consciousness by the unique combination of **substance** vibrations, we are now better able to understand that we can affect our *reality* by regulating that inner part of us, not necessarily changing the **substance** outside ourselves.

Whatever vibratory patterns impact our center of consciousness with the greatest **force** or clarity, that will be the *reality* of the moment for us. The *reality* in any case can have the same objectivity as that brought on through the common sensory faculties of our being. We need further to understand that our center of consciousness can be impacted at any time — while walking down the street, while being among a crowd of people, while resting comfortably at home, while working or playing, or while reading and writing.

Suggestion

Suggestion is usually initiated by ourselves or by the elements of our environment, often inadvertently. What other people say — or what signs along the streets and byways have to say — often have an effect on our thinking and are widely used by advertisers to influence our choice of goods and services. By our own preconceptions of things, we suggest to ourselves what things we will purchase, use or pursue. We usually have preconceptions of one kind or another about almost everything, and on that basis we often act.

Hypnotism

Formally, hypnotism is a suggestion from another person with an *intent* to alter our perception. A hypnotist can tell you that an onion on a table in front of you is an apple. If you allow yourself to be hypnotized, and if the hypnotist is well versed in his art, you may take a bite of the onion, and it will taste like an apple, without a doubt. Since his suggestion overrides the image vibrations which your eyes and nose bring to you, an apple will be the *reality* of the moment for you. You will *see* and *taste* an apple, and no one can tell you differently.

Habitual Responses

Habitual responses are the habit patterns in our mechanism which so strongly insert imagery into consciousness that they override the standard impressions brought in by the sense organs; they become the *reality* of the moment. For example, every evening you place your keys in a certain place, such as a night stand. Then one morning when you are ready to leave your residence, your keys are not in their usual place. You will swear that you put them in the usual place, and you will swear that you remember placing them there, at the usual time. In your mind's eye you can even see yourself doing it. It doesn't occur to you that you may have placed them somewhere else, and you begin asking around if anyone in the house took them from their regular place, for whatever reason. You may even search the house. But the sharp habit image in your consciousness is so strong that you just *know* that you put them there. Much distraught, you finally take spare keys from a cupboard and make your way to work. Sometime later in the day, when looking through your coat pockets, you find the original set of keys in the right hand pocket, exactly where you left them the night before. Some distraction at home kept you from following your usual pattern; you dropped the keys into your pocket, knowing that they would be secure and readily retrievable when needed.

Random Wave Patterns

Random wave patterns are the impulses which affect our perception in a manner other than the specific ways mentioned in the foregoing. These are wave patterns which we simply "pick up" from the countless waves of **substance** in which we live and have our being. They are non-directional. They are just "out there." The variables which bring them into consciousness needn't be detailed at this point, but they are part of the whole information package that is inherent in the System.

It will help if we repeat what we said of knowledge. All that there is to know, is the System itself. There is nothing existing which is not the System. Therefore, all that anyone can ever know is to know the structure and parts of the System. There is no knowledge beyond that. When we someday can be aware of every vibratory pattern in the **substance** of the System, we will have reached that point of knowing all there is to know. Whether or when we will reach that point remains to be seen.

Meanwhile, we need to remind ourselves that wave patterns are all around us. We need go no further than ourselves to discover what already is here and now. However, since our individual capacity to absorb and "learn" all these things in a lifetime is certainly limited, we need to utilize our human counterparts and the equipment we create to aid us in this vast undertaking.

Suffice it to say that when we receive thought impressions at random, they may simply be from the total storehouse of **substance** which surrounds us.

Memory Interference

Our conscious center is filled with data, memory patterns of what has passed. Each day of our lives, more and more data accumulates there. For the most part, the storage of data is well organized and is readily available when we need it. Memory is a key factor in intelligence, and it is primarily our memory capacity which places us at the forefront of other life forms.

While other life forms have a central nervous system and neural pathways feeding it data, the degree of capacity limits the number of messages which are handled in each species. A dog, for example, may very well *be aware* that it exists and be conscious of what is going on around it at any given moment, but the dog has little recall capacity to store and relate those events and those moments of self-consciousness into a unified thread of events. Repeated acts of the same kind may form habit patterns which regulate future responses, but not to the same degree that more memory would.

A concern we might have about memory is that it may overload with too much data. We don't know at this time what the capacities are for the different brains of the world's population, and certainly there are people with greater capacities than others, but overload would apply in either case. When there is overload, there is more chance that memory units will slip into consciousness and give us *reality* which is a past event, rather than current. Overload may also destroy existing memory units. It may merge units, thus giving us an incomplete or garbled recall image. Overload may also cause the "bleeding" of units packed too closely together, much as magnetic tape impressions can "bleed" from one tape to another when closely bonded over a period of time. This also would bring a mixed image.

Given all this, it can be expected that memory patterns have the potential of being a source of *reality* other than the norm.

Intuitive Flashes

These are the certain impressions we receive which are directly related to something in ourselves or in the people and things around us. They are true messages, in the way of hints, answers to questions, pictures, warnings, missing pieces in our problem-solving, or directions showing us which way to go. These flashes most likely result from momentary attunement with a specific area of **substance**, and often come in response to some wish or need which we have expressed, either openly or subconsciously.

It is not always easy to tell which of our flash impressions are the "real things," but there are ways in which one can learn to detect the meaningful from the non-meaningful. We learn to detect meaningful sounds out of the barrage of noise which besets us day in and day out; likewise, we learn to detect — out of the constant stream of light units which bombard us — vision patterns which are meaningful and related to us.

It takes, first of all, a knowledge of what is going on in perception, knowledge such as you are receiving now. Then, over a period of time, all hunches must be catalogued — sorting out, little by little, those which prove out and those which don't. As a beginning, a good rule of thumb is simply to dismiss the impressions which have no obvious meaning to you. It is fruitless to spend a lot of time trying to "discover" hidden meanings or symbolisms in them. If they have import for you, they will likely repeat themselves. It is better to keep your thoughts clear at these times, so that an understandable impression can follow.

We also need to guard against the tendency to believe that the impressions we receive are in any way a message "sent" to us by a disembodied being, divine or otherwise. Even though in our consciousness we may hear and see someone talking to us — such as a relative, a famous personage, or a fictional character — this is so only because any vibratory configuration of substance which impacts our consciousness takes on imagery of some kind.

This is not to say that there are no disembodied beings as such, for in a vibratory configuration, the universe abounds with potential imagery.

We can draw a parallel here to the presence of television transmissions which abound around us as vibratory configurations, each with its particular frequency. With a proper receiving set, we can tune in to these frequencies and receive an image. If someone seems to be talking to us directly, we know that that isn't the case.

So it is with our psychic perceptions. They seem so real to us at times, that we cannot help but believe that we were in direct contact with someone in a two-way conversation. It is no wonder that so many people think themselves specially selected for passing on a given message or directive from a great master or divine personage. Not only do we have to concede to the unlikelihood of this happening, we must also recognize that these messages may not be reliable, given the make-up of the perceptive process.

Our perceptions, from whatever source, are colored by the patterns and data already in our conscious center. Thus we read into many of our experiences something of ourselves, our predispositions, our leanings toward certain subjects or programs or designs, our basic likes and dislikes on a multitude of things. We are rarely *completely* open-minded and receptive to new material which comes our way.

This is another of Nature's properties which can make life less rosy than we would like it to be.

ELECTROMAGNETIC BEHAVIOR

Another of Nature's properties which can make life less rosy than we would like is its electromagnetic content, the **force** which drives its **substance**. **Force**, like **substance**, permeates Nature in all its parts. Without **force**, Nature would be in a vast stillness of non-manifestation. There would be neither waves to create imagery nor power to give life to the images. However, there *is* **force**, and because of **force**, there is Life.

Electromagnetism is a balancing factor in Nature, with its dual polarity. The plus and minus factors of its two poles are everywhere present. There are always the same number of plus and minus charges in the total spectrum of vibratory configurations, each with its potential for attracting or repelling the other. This attraction-repulsion behavior is sensed by the consciousness of life forms, and life forms respond to each other on the basis of either mutual attraction or repulsion.

Attraction and Repulsion

This attraction-repulsion quotient doesn't mean that a certain body is all positive and that something to which it's attracted is all negative. Each unit of Nature has just as much positive as it has negative; this carries over from vibrating **substance** to everything, from atoms to planets. Electromagnetically speaking, you are a balanced whole insofar as the degree of positive and negative charges is concerned. What makes a person as a whole a positive or negative person is the way in which all the little charges line up. Thus, when it is said that your right hand is positive while your left hand is negative, it simply means that all the little magnetic charges that make up you, as a unit of Nature, line up differently in each hand.

The following is a diagram of a bar magnet showing how this might work.

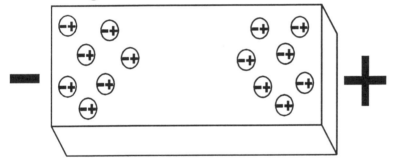

BAR MAGNET

The little circles represent atoms, each with its positive and negative charges.

Normally, in electromagnetic properties, a plus charge is attracted to a minus charge; thus balance is maintained. What makes life not so rosy, however, is that Nature, because of its motion, is always tending towards imbalance — toward a reversal of polarity in any given unit — while at the same time, the attraction factor is striving for balance again. Thus, while the motion of Nature confronts us with an ongoing tendency to get out of balance, we find that the electromagnetic forces are trying to bring balance back to any given situation.

When an imbalance proceeds unchecked for a period of time, the bringing about of a balance again often results in an upheaval such as we see in earthquakes, exploding stars or exploding people. Stress-release thus becomes a serious study in both physical and psychological sciences, and will undoubtedly be applied as successfully on people and their problems as it now is on architectural design.

Since electromagnetism is the moving force behind action in the make-up of Nature, it is also the moving force behind human activity. We can easily trace our behavior patterns to electromagnetic influences.

Following the Line of Least Resistance

For example, one of the characteristics of electromagnetism is its tendency to follow the line of least resistance. Throughout Nature, we can see the effects of this everywhere. The topography of earth's surface is marked by the winds and the rains doing just that. In human behavior, we can see the effects of this in our tendency to procrastinate, putting things off till tomorrow. Another is our tendency to take the easy way out. The easy way out often spawns such unwanted behavior as cheating, stealing and lying. Sometimes it may prove to be an economy of life. A common rationalization is the question, "Why do things the hard way when there's an easier way that gives the same result without hurting anything?" The problem with this line of thinking is that most often the "easier way" does hurt us and others. It is the parent of idleness and disregard for honest and forthright living.

As part of Nature, it is always with us, and presents us with an eternal challenge, a need to exert ourselves — to put forth work and effort, if we are to overcome. Nature is neither easy nor rosy.

Another characteristic of electromagnetism is its tendency to reverse its polarity in the dynamics of an undulating **substance**. This can be a source of much aggravation on the negative side, but on the positive side it brings about change. We don't like change much, as we will note later on, but change properly welcomed and measured, gives life and color and hope to what might otherwise be a drab life.

On the negative side, we see our moods change, more or less regularly, often without observable cause. We sometimes blame this state on such things as the weather or other people or our state of health. To make matters worse, we feel trapped and depressed when other people change their minds or completely reverse themselves on topics of interest or importance to us. We also see our likes and dislikes change. What attracts us one day may repel us a short time later. Over a period of time, people we like today may not appeal to us.

Polarization in Groups

Sometimes after an argument between ourselves and our adversaries, we may part, each holding to the original points of view. Then later, after some reflection, we may begin to modify our point of view and decide to admit this to our adversaries. Upon reaching them, before we can say anything, they may have done the same thing and stand talking about a new viewpoint — almost exactly what we had been saying all along. It seems an anomaly that we often dislike having others "come over to our side." If these others are more outspoken than we or have influence with highly-placed persons, they could end up taking credit for what was originally our idea. In any event, in world affairs, it seems that there are always opposing hemispheres. When any two reach agreement, a new set of oppositions will appear. This is Nature, forever polarizing, forever maintaining a balance by insuring a positive for every negative.

When we say that we are using psychology on someone, we're in effect manifesting that principle. If you want someone to do "something" for you, act as though that "something" is farthest from your mind. In fact you might make a point of saying, "No." Then you just sit and let Nature take its course.

Keep in mind that each of us is an electrically charged

mechanism with sensory apparatuses which detect the most minute variations in the electrical fields (auras) of people and things around us. As we move about, our auras brush the auras of thousands of different things each day. All this interaction — with our own auras and the auras of others — is subject to change at a moment's notice, giving us cause for many feelings during a day. Even if we stood still, we could not avoid sensing the changes in the motion of the **substance** around us.

In the face of a model of the universe so pre-set in its ways, so impelling and exciting, so overwhelmingly "in charge," what motivation remains for us — mere specks in an eternal verity? Much remains to be said about that.

Try to keep a proper perspective in all this. How important are we? In the larger picture, we are a blink of an eye. Within just a hundred years almost all of us will be dead and gone. That leaves Nature to go on for the next zillion years without us. Surely, that gives Nature some weight in having its say in the workings of things.

In the smaller picture, we, like any cog in the wheel, are as important to Nature's operations as anything else. We don't take time very often to emphasize the importance of cogs. They are too often overshadowed by the whole machinery of which they're a part, but they should always be given due credit by the "wheel," in any circumstance. Therefore, if at the moment you are a cog in some minor wheel, don't despair. You are important, and blessed humility can do wonders for you.

Sharing is fundamental to a state of harmony in society. It is folly for anyone to think that his/her achievements are due solely to his/her efforts, and to his/her efforts alone. If people do not share the fruits of their achievements with those who helped make them possible, then there will be a price to pay — sometime, somewhere, in one way or another.

If there is any goal toward which we can strive — a goal which will motivate us through hard times and good times, a goal which all can achieve, personally — it is an effort to harmonize with Nature. Get in step with its nuances, and be happy. Enjoy!

≡
4
≡

THE ENJOYMENT OF LIFE

Imperturbability: Our Ultimate Goal

What more meaningful and satisfying goal can we have in life, than to be at peace with ourselves and our surroundings? Knowing now that we cannot change Nature's law nor its structure, and knowing now what that law and structure are, there is a lot we can do in order to keep in harmony with them.

It is our nature to want permanency and stability in our lives. The Greek philosopher, Epicurs, described our desire for permanency and stability as a search for *imperturbability*, a state of living which is free of irritants and thus free of stress and conflict. He thought that this was the greatest good, the end of life.

This very much ties in with our previous discussion about Nature's ongoing process to find balance. From a system's point of view, imperturbability equates with balance, and we can use the terms interchangeably.

We're seeing more clearly now in what direction we're heading. In simplest terms, in order to achieve permanence and stability in our lives, all we have to do is to bring the elements of our lives into balance. In essence, that's the story. In practice, however, the great balancing act requires the utmost diligence and perseverance, for as we have clearly indicated, Nature does not make it easy for us. Against our natural desire to rest, Nature, by the very motion of its intrinsic energy, prods us ever more to move on.

Since our philosophy of life has a lot to do with the way in which we meet this challenge, let's now take a look at that subject.

All of us have a philosophy of life which is usually brought into play when we are in a decision-making situation of one kind or another. Our whole legal system is based on a system of courts of law in which judges are making decisions day in and day out, based in part on their philosophy of life. We cannot truly say that any of us, including judges, are unbiased in our judgments. We may believe that they are simply making judgments based on the letter of the law, but the very word, *judge*, indicates that their true function is *to judge* not only the severity of a criminal act, but also the severity of the punishment alloted. Moreover, these judgments sometimes vary widely between members of the profession.

Our philosophy of life is the way we look at life, the reasons for life being what it is, the reason for things happening as they do. If, for example, we believe that life is a dog-eat-dog existence, that it's the survival of the fittest, that it's everyone for himself, then that's the way we're going to live: selfish, taking care of ourselves first, being ruthless, and ignoring the common good. Or, for example, if we believe that there is universal justice, that as we sow, so will we reap, then we're going to be more careful about how we act toward the life around us. If we believe that through prayer we can have forgiveness for any wrongdoing, then we will act in still another way; if we are superstitious, we will act according to what the penalties are said to be for the countless superstitions that abound. In short, how we look at what is right and wrong depends upon our own philosophy of life.

Our philosophy of life thus has a great deal to do with

our state of *imperturbability*, or lack of it. If our philosophy of life is on track, we are going to achieve the imperturbable state. If it's not on track, we're in trouble. Being on track means that your philosophy matches the true state of BEING. It matches the rules and requirements of Nature. It matches life as it really is.

Much of our philosophy of life is based on proverbs which we learned as children. In these formative first years of our lives, the proverbs were easy to understand "rules for living" and, for the most part, they reflected Nature's requirements for having a harmonious life. For example:

- a stitch in time saves nine;
- an ounce of prevention is worth a pound of cure; and
- don't put off till tomorrow what can be done today.

These three companion proverbs stress the importance of prevention, something at which we're not very successful. Our procrastinating nature is to put things off until they get out of hand and then expend time and energy repairing or rebuilding. This is a source of great waste in society.

There are other proverbs which speak of thrift, frugality and conservation.

- Don't put all your eggs in one basket.
- A bird in the hand is worth two in the bush.
- Don't cry over spilt milk.
- A penny saved is a penny earned.
- Put something aside for a rainy day.
- A friend in need is a friend indeed.

We can assume without much argument that most people subscribe to the time-honored message of their particular proverbs, believing that if they were followed, the world would be in much better shape that it is now. This only points up again that many of our problems are not a result of *not knowing* what to do, but rather a result of *not doing* it. Of course, in reference to a state of imperturbability, knowing what to do is half the battle, and in one way or another, many of us have come at least that far.

An example of this can be seen in a common health problem. If you had an awful ache or pain and had begun to worry a great deal about its probable consequences and then had a doctor tell you that it was only indigestion — well, that's half the battle. Then you would know that the pain was symptomatic of a minor, easily corrected ailment. For all intents and purposes, you would then become imperturbable, without concern or worry — even though the pain persisted. Another example would be the appearance of an unexplainable noise in the rear end of your car. Not knowing what the cause was, you might begin to imagine all sorts of things, like a wheel that's about to come off, or a rear axle about to drop, or something in your fuel tank. You not only worry about the potential danger in these, but also about the inconvenience of something happening far away from a service station, not to mention the potential expense involved. On stopping the car and making a casual inspection of the outside, you find that you had picked up a metal strip of some sort which had wrapped around an axle and was knocking against the inside of a rear fender. Not being able to remove it there, you drive on, still with the noise, but with relative imperturbability.

Acting on what we know, however, is the second half of the battle. If you do not act on the warning signs as illustrated in the foregoing, your imperturbability could be short-lived. Indigestion needs correction, first by defusing the pain now felt and second by being more careful about your eating habits. With that taken care of, your imperturbability is more secure.

Likewise, if you do not quickly stop at a service station to have the unwanted metal strip removed from your axle, it could cause actual damage, both to the fender and to the axle components.

Next in line for our consideration is the subject of *truth*. Permanent imperturbability depends upon our knowing the truth about ourselves and about the situation and things around us. The truth will make you free, it is said, and so it will. Let's look now at some of the ways we face it.

Chances are that you may already realize how difficult it is to get to the truth — not only to get the truth out of others, but also to admit to it within ourselves.

What are some of the general attitudes toward truth? Strangely enough, we have an innate resistance to it. When someone is telling you something which you believe might get you involved, your immediate response might be, "Don't tell me; I don't want to know." What you don't know can't hurt you. Right? Wrong! What you don't know *can* hurt you. When a dentist or a mechanic offers information about how you can get your teeth or your car in shape, you can be asking for some real trouble if you choose not to know.

Often we have a resistance to knowledge and a great tendency to rest with what we have. Once we accept something as truth, there is very little that can budge us from that idea.

What is an idea? Let's imagine that you're out on a hillside with a companion, overlooking the countryside. Below are green fields, trees, roads, houses, animals, cars and people. As you sit there, literally observing the world, you start thinking.

Your companion opines, "You know, I think the world is flat."

You both sit there, observing the world. Nothing changes. Then you venture an opinion: "I think the world is round."

You both sit there, observing the same scene. Nothing changes. Then your companion comes up with: "I believe that when I die, that's it. Poof! I'm a memory."

Nothing changes. Then you say: "Well, I believe in life after death, that life goes on and on, maybe eternally." Nothing changes.

What is the point here?

The point is this: what we think about BEING is not going to affect the true state of BEING one iota. Yet people's passions have been fired to the boiling point over a mere expression of ideas. There was a time when some thinkers suffered harsh and unreasonable torture for voicing their ideas.

Thomas Jefferson, a founding father and third President of the United States, said:

"There is no truth existing which I fear, or would wish unknown to the whole world."

Nevertheless, people sometimes resist listening to new ideas or thinking about them, because they fear upsetting something in which they believe. Most people are not ready to change their minds, no matter how open-minded they think they are. It is uncomfortable for them. It means changing their entrenched points of view. We prefer that things be cast in concrete, but nothing is. To have to change is upsetting. It is irritating, and any irritant puts us out of balance, and we don't like to be out of balance. We like peace of mind. We like *imperturbability*. We do not like to have our way of life threatened, especially by such a "terrible" thing as the truth! We don't like having our lives changed in any way, unless things get so bad for us that changing is more peaceful than not changing.

Darkness holds a certain fascination for us. Although few of us would admit to preferring darkness over light, there is something in the darkness of ignorance, despair or guilt which seems protective and comforting. In that darkness we risk no exposure to the possible hurts and disruptions which knowledge, hope or responsibility might bring.

Most of us have our dark areas, shadows from which we hesitate to emerge. We cling to our beliefs and notions, often for no better reason than that we are used to them. They serve our purpose, and we see little reason to change them or to subject them to question and rebuttal.

It is in our natures to neglect the strong and righteous elements of our lives. It is in our natures to ignore or flee from goodness and light. It has been said that we are enslaved by anguish. We are attracted to the gross and disruptive aspects of life. We run to see fires and accidents. We become engrossed in news of scandal, gossip, murder, or other tragedies, to the extent that the front pages of most papers carry little other than that. We find it easy to fade into darkness, to let others do our thinking for us, to have others shoulder our responsibilities. We pursue misery — mistrust — and doubt our inner urges.

What does all this say for our claim that *imperturbability* or *peace of mind* is our supreme goal — that everything we do has only that purpose in mind? If we believe the statement that everything that people do is for the purpose of feeling good or achieving *imperturbability*, why then do they seem to pursue misery?

This all boils down to a realization that there are two paths to *peace of mind*. One is a direct path; the other is meandering. One is permanent; the other is temporary. On the direct path, we face up to the responsibility, to the employment of our faculties for creative and productive purposes, to the true state of things. We strive and work to bring balance into our affairs and into the affairs of those around us. We tend the flame. We take up the cross. We *earn* peace of mind, and what we receive for this effort is real contentment, real happiness, *imperturbability*.

On the meandering path, we tend to escape responsibility, putting off to tomorrow what could be done today, because *momentarily*, that is the easier way. We let our faculties lie dormant — not taking the time and effort to exercise, study, communicate — because *for the moment*, that is the easier way. We make no effort to right a wrong and no effort to bring harmony back into our environment; we stay at rest, and for a time enjoy the peace of idleness and lethargy. We let the flame die out. We pick up no crosses. The effort is too much for us. We find our peace in sitting and watching. We have our *imperturbability*. What we receive for this lack of effort, however, is boredom, insecurity, ill health, strife, and darkness, and the peace quickly vanishes into the night. Then it's a matter of starting over again, doing things the right way — next time.

We must always be conscious of the temptation to stray from the direct path. We don't like change any more than the next person. We look forward to our moments, our days, perhaps our years of rest, and often we find ourselves resisting change. We often feel that we would like to cast in concrete what we now have. While tending the flame of truth and righteousness, how often do we wish we could spend just one day, one night, without having to get up to add more fuel to the fire?

But the dynamics of universal motion push us on, and like many others, we *know* that there is no letting up, that there is not a time when we no longer have to be on watch, not a time when we will not be tempted, not a time when we no longer need to reinforce our commitments with daily or weekly reminders. When one goal is reached, when one task is done, there is another, and if there is not another waiting, we should seek one.

For real *imperturbability*, it is necessary to be busy, to be creative, to bring variety, change and excitement of a positive nature into our lives.

At this point it will be helpful to review the properties of **force**, as they are brought to bear on the subject of *imperturbability*.

The electromagnetic nature of BEING brings into all its phases the familiar pushing and pulling effect of opposing polarities. In more human terms, it accounts for the attraction or repulsion we feel toward all things, animate or inanimate. Since all things — every element of our total being — are polarized, the entire aspect of our relationship to the world around us is governed by the magnetic fields of our **substance**. Our moods, our behavior, our activities — voluntarily or otherwise — are determined by the polarity and the strength of the polarities around us. Electromagnetic forces account for all events of our lives, as we have seen, and in our play with life we must abide by the rules imposed by these forces. This means, for one thing, modulating the ups and downs of life into a more steady and balanced experience. The polarization of electromagnetism is often referred to as positive and negative polarization. These are purely technical terms and should never be interpreted as good or bad, constructive or destructive, but simply as opposites. We do not look at the poles of a magnet as being different in kind, but only in direction, and even that difference is relative to everything around it. A polarized condition which is attracting one thing could at the same time be repelling another thing. The ultimate behavior of things is determined by the relationship of their polarities to each other.

It is important to emphasize here that in the electromagnetic system, it is *opposites* which attract. How do we resolve this with our usual desire to associate with someone of like mind, as in "birds of a feather flock together"? Simply recall a previous statement: opposites, in polarity, do not represent goodness or badness; they are merely opposites. By the matching of two opposites, there is the ultimate balance, the ultimate fulfillment. Both opposites can have common goals in life, common backgrounds, common experiences, common interests. Together they combine their opposition into a more tolerant, balanced view of their common denominations.

Polarization is natural to the universal system. There is a constant and equal division of the whole into two poles, so that there is never more positive than negative in the total scheme of things. It is for this reason that we can have a system of mathematics, a science completely centered around the equals (=) sign.

The equals sign enters into both psychological and philosophical systems as well. For every cause there is an effect. The answer to questions in our mental make-up are as much dependent upon equating one thing with another as are the answers in scientific studies. In our feelings we are sensitive to imbalances in the life around us. An imbalance in our systems or in our relationships will invariably put us ill at ease, and thus we find ourselves constantly in search of balance. Balance brings *peace of mind*, or a sense of *imperturbability*, which to some philosophers has spelled the *summum bonum* of life, our individual and ultimate goal. In one way or another this is probably so. Behind all our urges and drives there is undoubtedly the one single drive to balance the equation, to satisfy a need to attain equilibrium.

People go to great lengths to achieve *imperturbability*. Much depends upon each person's understanding of what is needed to bring it about. Those who follow time-honored moral precepts are essentially living in accordance with the requirements of an electromagnetic system, for most moral codes are based on the Golden Rule, a yardstick of behavior which reflects a balanced approach to life. The mathematical equation is self-evident. There are persons who seek balance by revenge, doing unto others as others do to them. There are persons who try to insure *imperturbability* by gaining control of their environment, either the people in it or the things of the environment or both. They are attempting to insure long-term satisfaction of their needs. In doing this there is sometimes a tendency to overdo, thus causing an imbalance elsewhere, with the result that the perturbation of others will reflect back to them.

Balance is not an easy thing to maintain. Because of the inherent motion of BEING, there is continuing change in the composition of all vibratory patterns. As a result, we are obliged to shift and adjust, constantly, in order to keep in step or in balance with life's requirements. Nothing is at this moment exactly the same as it was a moment ago.

This necessity to adjust and change is a perturbation in itself, one which we often resist in our struggle to maintain balance and stability. We have a tendency to stay at rest, to maintain the status quo, to retire on the basis of past accomplishments. Yet the motion of life pushes on, carrying with it the constant need for adaptation. We can resist the push, but we will be buffeted about and left completely out of tune with the tempo of the time. On the other hand, by going with the rhythms of life, we experience smooth sailing, riding the crest of life to ever new vistas and experiences.

The most overriding irritant we face in our search for *imperturbability* is *change*, for it is always present, compelling us to alter, correct, adapt, or build anew on the many physical and spiritual structures which compose "our" world. Add to that our innate resistance to change and you have the makings of an eternal conflict between people and their environment.

Since change is such a major irritant, and since

change is forced upon us by the inherent motion of life itself, what chance do we have to ever achieve the imperturbable life?

One answer is to fully understand the *motion of life*, to know what kind of phenomenon we are considering; then we can set ourselves to the task of interfacing our lives with the natural rhythm of the phenomenon. The attainment of harmony with Nature is what we are addressing in this text.

No one should assume that the nature of life is horribly complex and well beyond the comprehension of mere mortals. On the contrary, the nature of life is incredibly simple and easily comprehensible to an open mind. Yet the nature of knowledge is such that people do not always welcome it with open arms, much less an open mind. Knowledge too, is something to which we have an innate resistance.

Why shouldn't we want to know? Why shouldn't we want to know everything we can? The answer: because knowledge is a harbinger of *change*. We cannot *know* without something changing within us. Once we know, we are almost always put into a position of having to act on what we know. We incur new responsibilities. We invite work and effort. We are nudged from a state of rest to a state of activity. If we do not act on what we know, we incur a sense of guilt, a sense of failure born of nonperformance. In either case, we suffer the pangs of perturbation. Therefore, we often elect to *not know*.

If you are in any way overwhelmed or intimidated by knowledge, keep in mind that the store of human knowledge today is nothing more than the recorded results of someone's observations. You, as an observer, are looking out at the same universe which every person before you looked upon. You are in the same position as were any of the great thinkers of the past. Since our vast storehouse of knowledge today is nothing more than the ideas, opinions, or conclusions of human observation, it is important that you realize that you are equally an observer, equally able to form ideas, opinions or conclusions on a par with all others in this respect. You are a starting point.

In all of this, we are not forgetting the value and benefit of others' ideas. They are not to govern your thinking, however, but to supplement your own ideas for a fuller understanding of life.

Directions – Options For Change

Change imposes still more requirements on us as we seek to achieve the imperturbable state. Our natural indecisiveness meets no greater challenge, perhaps, than when we have a choice of direction. We have seen that change is the order of the day, but *when* do we change and *how often* do we change?

It is important, first of all, to review what change is all about. What changes? Does everything change? Are changes actual or superficial? There are some things that do not change, and one of these is the source of our real world. The *actuality* that is our universe does not change in its basic make-up. Its manifestations and appearance change to us, but its basic parts do not. There are several analogies which we can make to illustrate this.

Let us say that *light* is part of *actuality*. It has a fundamental characteristic; it is the result of a basic universal wave-length. But light never shows itself to us as a single thing, perhaps never as its *actual* nature. We see it in countless shades and in countless hues. These hues and shades are constantly in a state of flux, for light is vibratory, and as one vibration touches our eyes and passes on, another takes its place, reflecting from an ever so slightly modified version of the source.

A kaleidoscope may prove to be another good example. The brilliant pieces of plastic and glass retain a basic identity, a basic shape, a basic color and texture in their *actual* state, but to the eyes looking through the pieces, the basic shapes assemble themselves in a constantly changing array of patterns. The units of plastic or glass do not change, essentially, but in the motion given to them by an operator, the aspect visible to the observer is one of change. The kaleidoscope can also serve as an example to better understand the seeming appearance of new shapes or new species, as the development of a planet unfolds.

We can take some comfort in the fact that the basic universe is an infinite principle, the same yesterday, today and tomorrow. **Substance, mind, force**, the motion or vibration of **substance**, the push and pull of positive and negative polarities — these are all universal constants, and for all intents and purposes, they do not change.

In effect our consciousness stands still, while waves of **substance** pass by us in ever changing patterns. Adjusting to this change of patterns is what we often resist, and the need to adjust is the sometimes irritating characteristic of sentient existence. It is as though we were standing in a sea, conscious of the waves which pounded past us. The ever changing pattern of the waves — the highs, the lows, the tugging, pulling, pushing — causes us concern as we try to keep our balance, with our head above water. We welcome any still interlude where we are not required to struggle to remain standing.

In this illustration, the water is a constant. Its basic nature remains unchanged; it is the patterns to which we adjust our consciousness, not the water. The concern of the person standing in the sea is not to go with or against the sea, but only to work with or against its patterns.

We can see in this discussion that we are illustrating inertia, one of the primary parts of Isaac Newton's dynamics. Inertia is another way of describing the manner in which we tend to cling to what we have or to continue on whatever path we have chosen to travel. Why? We have a resistance to change, for change is perturbation — in other words, we resist because of inertia. A resistance to change keeps us in our ruts; inertia keeps us in our ruts. This applies, of course, whether our ruts consist of *doing nothing* or *doing something*.

Other dimensions of dynamics fit together with the principle of electromagnetic **force**, as we have outlined it.

Gravity is a powerful attracting force, as is magnetism.

The action and reaction of physical elements is the universal balancing act caused by the polarization of elements.

Inertia reflects the tendency of elements to stay in balance, either by following a line of least resistance or staying at rest until moved by some event or other.

The dynamics of the universe are what move us, and the basic principles of dynamics are worthy of study and application to our lives. They are part of Universal Law, and affect everything we do. They are the law of our being and are evident everywhere in our environment. The choice is to work with the sea or against it, as our illustration shows.

If we look at life the same way, it is not a question of going with or against life and its inherent nature. Rather it is a matter of adjusting to the patterns of existence which life offers us — patterns which are constantly in a state of flux relative to our consciousness. The motion of the universe, as the motion of the sea, provides us with ever-changing patterns — with highs, lows, tugging, pushing and pulling — and it is to this that we have to adjust.

Adjusting doesn't always mean taking a particular direction. Adjustment can often mean just an adaptation of consciousness to what is happening. As the tide rolls in or out, it isn't always a question of going with the tide or against it, but often just a mental adjustment to stand "cool" and observe it coming and going with equanimity. If we want more excitement than that, then a choice of going with the tide must anticipate a recession of that tide, a drifting back to a starting point. This offers a complete cycle of adjustment and a world of experience and excitement as well. Those who go with the tide and are ready and prepared to slide back with the tide are well adjusted, having taken command of themselves. Those who stand still have assumed a kind of adjustment, but it is short of experience. Those who go against the tide are always fighting an uphill battle; those who go with the tide and then stand still, find themselves out on a limb, out of the mainstream, and their sense of adjustment falls short.

The persons with the greatest advantage, of course, are those who know all about nature and the motion of life — a state of knowledge to which all should aspire. This doesn't relieve them from their place in the sea of life, but it does give them a complete set of options for dealing with life and knowing what they can expect from it, what consequences they incur by various actions on their part. Nothing will change the nature of life; nothing will cease or alter its eternal motion; but people can adjust to its changing configurations to suit their frame of consciousness. They can live in both extremes, from complete maladjustment with its battering and suffering, to complete adjustment with its equanimity and pleasure.

As to previous questions of *when* we change, and *how often* we change, we should guide ourselves by several general rules. We should always be ready to change when common sense or the requirements of our environment necessitate it. We should initiate change in those things when, with foresight, we can see that change is inevitable. We should change from that which has served its usefulness to that which will be more useful. Remember: that which we discard and that which we pursue are both units of BEING, and both have their place in the complete cycle of change. We should change when we believe that change will improve our lives. We should not let hesitancy or fear prevent us from leaving familiar ground for that which is less familiar — that which our reason and senses have indicated is better for us.

We should not change for the sake of change. We should not change simply because the surge of our environment is toward change. Rather, we should adhere to our own good sense, which sometimes means standing fast against popular trends and opinions. We should not change if we do not feel like changing. Again, everything is part of BEING, and there is no way we can go anti-BEING. We may go anti-pleasure, anti-good for ourselves, anti-anything, but not anti-BEING. If we want to stand still it is our prerogative, and if we are happier that way, all well and good. We must watch against being pressured into things we really do not want to do, assuming that the results of our decision affect us and us alone. When we get in someone's way deliberately by our refusal to change, then we should let those who want to change go by.

The final judgment is an intuitive one. It is difficult to set up objective standards as to when people should change and when they shouldn't. Not only is each case separate and distinct from any other, but there is always the option of whether a person wants to change or not, even if changing would be for his own good.

The *how often* of change is, of course, tied in with the *when.* Change as often as you want, if you are an adjustable person. As we stated earlier, go back and forth with the tide every day if you wish, or just go occasionally, or don't go at all. You could be right in every case.

As a last word, we emphasize that shifting direction regularly enlarges your realm of experience and your capacity to understand and cope with the movement of the sea around you.

> "Rest is not quitting the busy career;
> Rest is the fitting of Self to its sphere."
> — J.S.Dwight

A Time For Letting Go

Being unable to let go is one of the greatest handicaps which individuals face in life. We have a tendency to cling to ideas, to possessions, to friends and relations — a baby to its rattle, a boy to his girlfriend, a man to his political convictions, a mother to her children. More damaging than these is our clinging to negative experiences. We harbor feelings of disgust, hate, envy or revenge, for anything — from the way people look at us to the suffering we undergo from a wrong perpetrated on us by thoughtless drivers who impede the flow of traffic by their slow reaction to signal lights or the movement of cars ahead of them. There always seems to be something happening to us during the course of a day which we continue to "chew on" inside ourselves, feelings which sometimes stay with us for hours or days.

There is a time-honored principle which ties in with this, and that is *forgiveness. Forgiveness* is, in effect, a *letting-go*; as such, it has been a major consideration in our moral codes. Clinging to things is often justified on the basis that it is a mark of stability, constancy, single-mindedness, loyalty and saving; similar practices have been regarded as virtues by a society intent on preserving the *status quo*. These qualities unquestionably have their place in the whole picture of life, but for perfect harmony and compatibility, they must be mitigated by regular and periodic adjustments.

When we view BEING as a dynamic, vital entity, always in motion, the vibrations which at any moment give you an impression of a sound or color pass on, and other vibrations take their place. Since we know a thing by its vibratory pattern, a thing is constantly changing as the vibratory pattern changes. Each new vibratory pattern which makes us aware of a thing is a change from the one before it. Thus we say that everything is in a constant state of change. Nothing is at this moment the same as it was the moment before. This applies also to ideas. As soon as we conceive an image, it begins to undergo change. In a few days, in a few weeks, or in a few years, we may no longer recognize an idea that we originally held, even though we may think that it has not changed in our consciousness.

We live in a universal system in which change is the order of the day. Universal patterns, the vibratory configurations of **substance** which give us our images of things, are constantly in a state of flux, moving from one pattern into another. The Universe moves, and if we are to stay in step and synchronize with this movement, we must move with it.

Most people acknowledge this. Acknowledging it, however, doesn't change the tendency to cling to what has passed. This is because we have an innate resistance to change, a form of inertia which keeps us remaining in repose while the rest of the world moves on. Why such a paradox in our make-up?

The paradox arises out of the intrinsic structure of BEING. BEING itself is a system of paradoxes, by our standards. It has an ebb and a flow. It has opposing directions in its dual polarity, one which attracts and one which repels.

Attraction and repulsion are consequences of the electromagnetic system of BEING. These forces are constantly at play; they cause the dynamism — and often the great convulsions — of nature. As part of the structure of BEING, we are subject to this eternal play of forces, and with the attribute of consciousness, we are sensitive to them. As it happens, however, we only experience a sense of pleasure when we are caught up in an attraction to something. When we are thrown into situations which repel us, we have a sense of discomfiture. Thus we have our periods of highs and lows, of exultation and depression. Since our consciousness finds depression distasteful, we tend to avoid it. We strive to hold onto our highs, to those things which give us pleasure. There we have the first incident of resisting change. We do not want to change from that which gives us pleasure.

Yet there is no single pleasure situation which is permanent. Any pleasure situation will turn into pain if we cling to it and refuse to let go, for the motion of the universe will in due course present us with an opposite polarity in any given situation, in spite of ourselves. What attracts us at one moment may repel us the next.

To illustrate this, visualize some common pleasures. When you are hungry, the satisfaction of that hunger through eating begins as pleasurable pursuit. In terms of harmonics, we can say that you are strongly attracted to the food. As you go on eating, however, the attraction quotient diminishes and you become less attracted to the food. If we carried the illustration far enough — let's say eating to the point of discomfiture — the food would lose its attraction; in fact, you could be repelled by it.

In another illustration, imagine that you were looking forward to getting out in the fresh air, just to lie in the sun on a balmy day. You feel that you could just lie there forever, in peace and ultimate contentment. But after several hours, the sun would be too warm, the prone position too uncomfortable, the fresh air no longer seeming so intoxicating. Again, carried to the extreme, the whole situation could eventually repel you.

If a hot shower attracts you, only so much time will elapse before the running water annoys you, and you will wish to get out and dry off.

Those who find pleasure in reading or listening to music or engaging in charitable deeds will find that the attraction point in any given situation has its terminus, that there is nothing that can be enjoyed forever, at least not without a break.

Now we've reached the point to be considered. In order to maintain the pleasure quotient in all of our daily situations, we must never run any pleasure into the ground. We must be ready and willing to let go, at the appropriate time, so that the things which attract us now will continue to be attractive in the future. We must practice moderation in our pursuit of pleasure, and when we feel the pull — the impelling urge toward a person, a situation, an idea, or a hobby — we must exercise a degree of restraint, using our mind power to set limits for us so that we control our destiny within the ebb and flow of the universal tide. This is the path to harmonious living.

You now have a special insight into the ways of BEING, and with this knowledge, you can adjust and maneuver yourself into reasonably pleasurable situations as a way of life. You can change before the motion of the universe forces you to change. You can get off your chaise lounge before the prone position and the height and light of the sun begin to bother you. You can look for an alternative which will attract you in the interim. You can stop eating before you are disenchanted with food. You can keep from imposing yourself on your loved ones to the point of disaffection. You can keep from overdoing anything. You can change before you are asked — or forced — to change, and in this you will come close to finding eternal pleasure. You will learn to know that letting go is not the end of the world. Actually it is a threshold to new worlds, each as beautiful and full of promise as the old.

As we travel through the conscious state, there is no end to the conditions which can give us pleasure, for BEING is always phasing between that which attracts and that which repels. One handicap we have is that we may deny ourselves this vast reservoir of endlessly pleasurable experiences by not freeing ourselves from situations which have passed their peak and will only draw us into the repulsive, depressive phase of BEING's ebb and flow.

5

ENLARGEMENT OF
PREVIOUS DISCUSSIONS ON
SIGNIFICANT SUBJECTS

Extrasensory Perception

One reason that we are dwelling again on the nature of perception and a definition of *reality* is to have the process registered in your mind's eye, so that the next step is easier to understand. This step is the *actuality* which we realize through extrasensory perception. By referring back to the illustration in which an individual is depicted in the process of perceiving an apple, we recall that the apple can be perceived either through the familiar sense faculties or through the less familiar extrasensory faculties. Although we intimated that certain glandular centers may act as sensory organs in cases of extrasensory perception, the exactness of that possibility is not important for the point we wish to make. In whatever way the extrasensory perception reaches our center of consciousness, the important thing to understand is that it does reach there. It reaches there through some kind of sensory apparatus, and when it gets there, we *realize* it in the same frame of reference as we realize the impressions coming through the familiar sense faculties — feeling, smelling, seeing, hearing or tasting.

We explained previously that the lower degree of clarity with which these impressions come through is probably due to the fact that the extrasensory faculties are secondary faculties in the average person. On the other hand, where these faculties are developed, a person can use them with equal facility, obtaining clear and meaningful impressions from both sources.

Of most significance, however, is the fact that when an extrasensory impulse comes through with clarity, it causes the center of consciousness to realize it in the same three-dimensional *reality* in which it realizes impressions coming through the familiar sense faculties.

Only persons who have had an extrasensory experience of this kind can verify how "real" the experience is. It is the same as any normally objective experience. If it is visual, they "see" the experience against the backdrop of their normal visual experience; sometimes it completely overrides the normal sense stimulus, and is the whole *reality* for the moment. Though such vivid experiences are had by relatively few persons, there are other extrasensory experiences which are more common. There are many persons, perhaps yourself included, who have heard sounds or sensed odors or felt a "presence" in the absence of any obvious external cause for such sensation. The "hearing" of a sharp voice or sound just when awakening or at the terminus of a dream is an example of how an extrasensory stimulus to your conscious center will manifest as *sound*, just as readily as an ordinary sensory stimulus.

To keep this understandable, always go back to the original illustration depicting sensory impressions, remembering that even with normal objective perception, we do not "hear" or "see." Rather, we *perceive* sounds and sights as a result of an electric-like stimulation passing along nerve fibers to our conscious centers. There, as a result of these electric-like stimulations, we realize *sound* or *sight* or other sense activities. Thus, to create sounds or sights from other sources, all we have to do is reproduce the same kind of electric-like stimulation, which in effect is what an extrasensory impulse does.

It is very important that the nature of extrasensory impressions be understood, for it is vital to the mental health of the individual that the extrasensory impressions are evaluated in their true perspective. To encourage the development of extrasensory awareness without an understanding of its nature — without regard to its possible disturbing effects on the individual — is an irresponsible practice. Uncontrolled and misunderstood extrasensory awareness has driven many people to a point of extreme mental disorder, for they had no way of coping with another *reality*. Some individuals have by birth a somewhat developed extrasensory faculty. They often "see" and "hear" things which, obviously, others cannot see or hear. If the "extra-perceptive" individuals don't understand what is happening — if they cannot control or sort out the impressions which come through the extrasensory faculties, if the faculties are like an open door which they cannot open and shut at will — they will almost certainly experience mental and physical breakdowns. It seems that such persons are also more sensitive to the emotionally-charged experiences of life, experiences that can range from violence to exhilaration.

If you can imagine not being able to sleep because you cannot shut out sounds or sights — not being able to eat or deal with your daily responsibilities because of the constant presence of images which frighten or disturb you — you will have some idea of what these individuals go through. Such abnormal experiences could be due to a physical aberration; as such, they must be considered in a physical sense on the same terms as a tumor, blood clot, or other aberration which would obstruct the normal flow of sensory impulses.

Persons who use any kind of artificial stimulants to arouse their extrasensory faculties are opening themselves to the same kind of mental disorder. If done too frequently, the result could be permanent damage to the control of extrasensory imaging and a consequent loss of contact with the norm. Persons who induce such hallucinatory experiences with stimulants are also endangering their lives, for when they are "seeing" something that isn't there, they also are *not seeing* something which *is* there, as in the case of the intoxicated man who ran off the highway. What he "saw" was the highway curving in front of him; he didn't see that the highway actually continued on in a straight line.

We must distinguish here once again between the two sources of *reality*. The extrasensory experience can be just as real as the normal sensory experience. Often it is the *reality* of the moment for the person having the experience, but its source is a different frequency band of **substance** and is not in sequence with the frequency band which makes up the normal world of *reality*. An extrasensory experience, such as the curve in the highway, had an actual source in a **substance** vibratory pattern. It is so for all our thoughts, imaginations and dreams. However, these **substance** patterns are not in the same time-space sequence as those with which we deal in our normal sensory state. Thus, though the curve in the highway was indeed an image in the person's consciousness — and it was just as real as the highway image coming through the normal sense faculties — still the image source of the curve was not from the same source as the one on which the car was moving; consequently an accident ensued.

Our entire life experience occurs within a given frequency band of **substance**. Within that band there is a sequential order which provides us with the potential for a reasonably harmonious life. Our sensory faculties can guide our bodies along a path which keeps them free from injury and ill health. We have the means, generally, within the order of our existence, to maintain a balanced and imperturbable life. Our physical bodies, which are essential to our identity of self, are geared to the rules and laws of the **substance** band which makes up our physical world. Our bodies are affected by fluids, solids, gravity and pressure, and the health of our bodies depends upon living in harmony with these laws. If we ignore this relationship and escape too often into hallucinatory experiences, the body will suffer and deteriorate to the extent that it no longer can serve as a carrier or agent for the working of **mind**. Thus **mind**'s ability to be aware or act will be correspondingly diminished and ultimately terminated.

As a free agent, you are free, of course, to hallucinate whenever you wish. Fantasizing is another form of hallucinating, although it is usually less vivid. Fantasizing in controlled and positive areas can be enjoyable, creative and therapeutic, and there certainly is nothing wrong with it as such. A person should be careful, however, to fantasize only when in a quiet or still position — not while driving a car, moving about, or being busy at work. Fantasizing should be *used* by a person as other forms of relaxation or entertainment are used, when a person is ready and to the extent that he is in control. In fantasizing, one can draw on both the extrasensory faculties and the imagery already recorded in the conscious center. Fantasizing should be a normally developed mental faculty. When it is induced by drugs, liquor or other stimulants, it is in danger of getting out of control. When it is thus induced, there is also the danger of injury to the physical structure, the consequences of which we have already discussed.

A question posed by all of the foregoing is this: How do you know which *reality* is the norm? At any given moment in time, you don't know. When we are subject to extrasensory realities, we generally need time to sort them out from the norm. This we can usually do within a short time after; extrasensory impressions are generally transient, lasting for only a brief period. After they pass, we can verify the extrasensory experiences by comparing them to what was going on in the normal *reality* at that time. As an example, if in the middle of a crowd you "saw" someone you knew quite well, but you later found out for a certainty that the person was a thousand miles away at that time, you would be verifying that your "seeing" him in that situation was an extrasensory happening. The same is true when you hear voices and you can verify that no one is around, or when you can smell the odor of incense when there is none anywhere near. Such delayed verification is of no help when you are confronted by an extrasensory impression to which you must react instantly, as the driver who suddenly "saw" a curve in the highway.

Extrasensory ability, at best, must be approached with caution. Unless it is absolutely under control — that is, manifests itself only on command — it easily can be disruptive and dangerous. Those who look at all extrasensory experiences as a divine mandate and follow those impressions implicitly are lending themselves to serious emotional problems. The usual extrasensory experience is still a random sampling out of the multitudinous wave patterns of **substance** which surround us. Many have no meaning or relationship to our lives, and unless a meaning is more or less obvious, the impression should be discarded out of hand. This is a good rule of thumb for those persons who are concerned about the meaning of dreams or of their so-called psychic experiences.

The positive side of extrasensory perception is in its potential for greater awareness. The basis of all education is greater awareness, the idea being that the more you are aware of a certain thing or condition, the more easily you can cope with it. The more information you have on a subject, the more correctly you can make judgments regarding the subject. Extrasensory perception can give us that extra measure of awareness and information when the perceptive faculties are properly trained and directed.

In this frame of reference we will discuss the phenomenon of *intuition*. Intuitive information, by our definition, is essentially the information which we draw from our extrasensory faculties. The extrasensory faculty can sense vibrations of things that normally are imperceptible to us. It can be aware of subtle traits and potentials that lie beneath the obvious, beneath the objective form and behavior of a thing. When you combine the intuitive sense with your other sense faculties, you are sensing more of the whole object under consideration.

In the illustration on the next page, there is a man shopping for a tree. With his eyes, perhaps with his touch, he is aware of the tree's form and general appearance. Normally he would make his judgment on the basis of this information. It looks sturdy and healthy and it feels solid and strong. What lies inside its structure, however, would

be hard to determine. What is its hereditary weakness, and how would it grow in the spot where it is to be planted? These would be hidden factors in the tree's true value. The intuitive sense could give the man extra assurance — that extra information which would make him feel with certainty that a given tree is the tree for him. The intuitive sense would utilize the known, but indiscernible, vibratory patterns of the tree — of the spot where it was to be planted, of the care that would be given it and of the purpose for which he wanted the tree.

A discussion of ESP almost always brings up the subject of precognition. These are perceptions of events, in clear detail, which have not yet occurred in our normal time frame but which occur sometime in the future of this time frame. Because of personal experiences of many people, myself included, we can be quite certain that they exist.

For example, a friend of mine was driving along a stretch of highway, when suddenly a truck came out of a side road not far ahead. He applied his brakes, but could never have stopped in time if the truck had been real. But it was not. The "vision" disappeared almost as quickly as it had come; there was no side road or truck apparent to him at that point. Just a quarter-mile further on, however, there was a side road with a large bank almost shielding it from view. As my friend approached it, now having slowed almost to a stop, the very image of the truck in his "vision" pulled out in front of him. There, however, the truck was far enough away and my friend was going slowly enough to avoid a collision.

There are many reported instances of people who have had strong feelings about their safety if they were to embark on a given voyage or simply leave their homes at a given time. We could say that the intuitive faculty is simply the sensing of known factors — things which already exist and which would come through, as a single message, into the consciousness process.

It is another way in which intuition serves to guide or warn us of impending circumstances; given certain known factors, these circumstances are inevitable.

Nature tends to be cyclic in its manifestations, owing in part to its acting upon itself rather than proceeding "ever onward" in a straight line. Such cycles as the tides, the seasons or the orbiting planets are examples of recurring events. We see cycles everywhere, and for every cycle we can see, there are doubtless many unseen and many still unmeasured. Intuition could sense the onset of a cyclic recurrence and help us to "predict" a future event.

You would enjoy this same advantage with regard to any judgments or purchases you may have to make. In your human relationships, you could pick friends, associates or intimates with a great deal more insight into their inner personalities. In deciding which way to go when a decision confronts you, you are prepared to make the right decision. When you want to make a trip, you can more easily decide when and how to go. The intuitive sense not only adds greatly to your awareness of a subject, but it adds to that awareness a sense of knowing how to treat the subject. The person who combines the intuitive sense with the normal senses makes few mistakes, and as a result has a greater potential for a full and complete life.

The development of the intuitive sense requires exercise and use of the sense over a period of time. During the training and exercise period, its use should be applied to non-critical areas of your life; depending upon it should come only after its use is consistently proven effective in your dealings with others.

Mind Power

What is **mind** power? What can mind do in the way of affecting material things? Can mind alone move material objects in the normal, objective, sense of the word? Can it lift chairs, carry people from one place to another, materialize something out of nothing or give wings to heavy objects? Can it produce chemical changes, create physical barriers or heal the sick? Can it "read" the thoughts of others or perceive things that are hidden?

The popular cliche, "mind over matter," is generally used in connection with the thinking processes — the ability of the mind to think through problems and thus surmount material obstacles. If a person comes upon a seemingly insurmountable problem such as a sticky cap on a new jar of jam, his first impulses are to exert greater physical force on the cap, even to using tools if necessary. Soon he will have out pliers, wrenches, vises and "what have you" in order to force the sticky cap to move.

There are other ways to loosen the cap, however. By giving thought to the matter, it may be discovered that softening the sticky substance which is holding the cap will loosen it. So by holding the jar under hot water for a moment or two, the cap does indeed loosen and can be turned almost effortlessly.

Those who take the cliche "mind over matter" more literally conceive of mind performing such supernormal processes as lifting great stones without any physical force being applied. From such concepts have come the legends that the huge building blocks of the pyramids were lifted into place by mental levitation, that the ancients physically traveled from one place to another by mind power, that they had the means of willing things to happen (such as willing the destruction of their enemies).

People who accept these legendary concepts at face value do not stop to realize the implications which they carry. If mind can indeed exercise such power, then why bother, in the case of the pyramids, with a building process at all? Why not simply have the pyramids shape themselves out of the rock of the quarries, complete with tunnels, chambers, and handcrafted decorations? If mind can nullify gravity, why bother with airships or vehicles? Why not just lift yourself and whatever you want to transport to wherever you are going? If mind can will the destruction of your enemies, why can it not will that you have no enemies at all? One should be as easy as the other.

Furthermore, if matter could be affected by mind alone, think of what chaos could result. If the laws of attraction and repulsion could be put aside by the mere wishes or whims of man, there would be no order or stability in life, for at any time and at any place a person's desires could simply change the entire environment. You might work to build a bridge. (For that matter, why would you even work? You would simply levitate the parts of a bridge over a river.) Then another group would find it ugly, spoiling the scenery. With a wish, they would levitate your bridge into a junk heap far away. The whole world would be topsy-turvy.

Our clue to the possibilities of such a conception of mind power is again found in the macrocosm around us. Even Nature uses no such abortive power. Nature does not utilize mind power to upset the equilibrium of the material world. The mind of BEING follows the laws and principles of its nature. We might say, then, that the law is stronger than the **mind**. The law of BEING governs its actions and limits the direction and powers of its **mind**.

In one sense we can draw a comparison between **mind** and electricity. Electricity only manifests itself as light or power under particular circumstances. Otherwise, it is a **force** which lies just beyond such manifestations, ready to express itself wherever and whenever the proper conditions exist. The proper conditions in this case are the coming together of electrical generators and instruments such as lamps, heaters, engines.

Mind is manifest as consciousness or mind power only under particular circumstances as well. Otherwise it, too, lies just beyond such manifestation, ready to express itself whenever the proper conditions exist. The proper conditions in this case are the coming together of such elements as soul, body, and **force**.

We must keep in mind the fact that universal elements and forces act only in certain channels, and that without these channels no action is manifest.

Mind has a great deal of control over matter, however, within the limits of universal law. It can mold and alter the form of matter to suit its own designs. Mind is creative. It can conceive of new arrangements of matter and bring them into manifestation. It can search out and manipulate the structure of matter to satisfy countless goals. It can convey instructions and desires from one living thing to another.

There are two areas of mind power which should be emphasized; these relate to the extension of imagery and to the use of *will* to direct the affairs of our lives.

Through the use of will, mind power can be applied in various ways. It can transmit an image of an individual to distant places, with full knowledge on the part of a party or parties at the distant place. The extension of such imagery to the consciousness of another person can carry with it the full context of the personality of the individual; in such a case, the recipient can experience a so-called materialization or vision of the person who is extending an image. In this way one person can "appear" to others. This is the essence of so-called astral journeys, wherein the soul of man is thought to travel through some mysterious medium from one place to another. With this power, it is not necessary to think in terms of a mind power which will physically transport persons from one place to another or physically levitate them or physically let them walk through solid walls, because travel and visitations can be accomplished through the simple extension of imagery. Meanwhile, mind will devise more and more sophisticated ways of transporting "physical" objects through the application of natural laws.

Another of the great powers of mind is its ability to generate imagery. It can conjure up wave forms or thought pictures which can affect the mental and material affairs of your life through sympathetic attunement between your thought form and the object of the thought itself. With this power you can influence the thoughts of others. You can attract others to you. You can be attuned to the thoughts and wisdom of others for problem solving. You can attract yourself to those people or things which correspond with your thought patterns. **Mind**, with its power to build thoughts and to sense the harmonics between thoughts and things, can have real power in dealing with matter.

Categorically, let us take each of these under consideration. First, **you can influence the thoughts of others**. This does not mean that you can arbitrarily control other people. It simply means that your thoughts can be received by another person. The other person is still in control. The other person is still free to accept or reject thoughts, no matter what their source. Your thoughts, however, can be implanted through a process of attunement. They can be received by a person either vaguely or clearly, depending upon the receptivity of the person and upon the strength and clarity of your thought. To the receiving persons, the thought will come into their consciousness, just as the myriad of other thoughts pass through their minds each day. What effect it will have on them or what heed they will pay to it is solely dependent upon its meaningfulness to them. It must be remembered that harmful or negative thoughts are more destructive to the person holding them and trying to transmit them, than they are to the persons who have just a passing recognition of them.

One of the positive, constructive ways in which thoughts can influence others is in preparing people to listen to your appeal or point of view. Before going in for an interview, before proposing, before asking for favors, hold the thought of a favorable response in mind. Visualize that the person or persons to whom you hope to speak are being agreeable. When you finally approach them, they may have had some previous "feeling" about the interview, and since it ostensibly came out of their own thoughts, they will be more receptive to the idea.

A second power of mind is that **you can attract others to you**. Through mind power you can establish a condition in your aura that will bring people of like mind and like conditions into your environment. This we naturally do, anyhow, under ordinary circumstances, but the mind can very effectively control this condition and improve the life of a person to a great degree by bringing about changes through positive thinking. Positive attitudes — thoughts of love, peace, harmony — become a part of the aura and its attractive potential almost as soon as they are generated and held in the mind. Thus it is often said, "As we think, so we are."

A third power of the mind is that **it can attune the individual with the thoughts and wisdom of others** for inspiration and problem solving. A question or problem which is contemplated, visualized, then released, will find a response from **substance** as a whole or from some individual who has had experience with the same problem. The nature of the problem itself sets up a natural attunement with its possible solutions which exist in **substance** or in the thoughts of others. This process is probably the most frequently applied function of mind's special powers.

A fourth power of mind is in its ability to **establish an area of attunement between people and things**. Through visualization, you can be aware of places and people to approach in order to satisfy certain needs and desires. The attunement between your visualized images and the object of the images themselves will lead you to the object or situation, so that you can proceed from there.

For those who are looking for better jobs, new homes, good leads as to professional advice, sources of purchases for various things in their home and business, the last-mentioned use of mind power is especially applicable. By properly visualizing their need, they will find themselves being led to sources directly or to sources which will give them the information they want. They will be led to all the facts available for that particular need. They will have all the information, contacts, and sources they need to make a judgment or a proper purchase. (It is important to understand that you might get a negative response, a clear message that what you want isn't right for you, at least at that moment.)

These uses of mind power are the real issue when speaking of mind over matter, and the powers are relatively simply to use.

Mind and matter work hand in hand. Without anything of which to be conscious, or without anything to appreciate and direct, mind's existence would be a void. Having matter exist without mind to appreciate and use it would be equally futile. What we see is the happy blending of the two, and the final question should not be which is superior, or which has dominion over which, but rather a utilization of the full potential of both in one harmonious accord.

Soul – An Inner Self?

Fundamental to most philosophical systems is the concept of *soul*, an inner self which transcends most physical limitations and retains its inherent structure after the death of the body. The idea of *soul* is anathema to some philosophical schools, especially the mechanists and functionalists who hold that personality is simply a function of a mechanical system.

Nevertheless, I suppose nearly everyone believes they are, first and foremost, a soul. There is nothing in our "model" which would exclude that possibility, although not in the traditional sense — not as a loose, separate entity flying about here and there, independently conscious of itself and "living" in another plane similar to this one after death. It is understandably difficult for us to understand "invisible" things as having such properties as identity or memory, but our television technology is showing ever more clearly how wave configurations are a basis for *reality*. Just as in communication transmissions there are invisible carrier waves which have on them imprints of voice and imagery, so can soul — having a universal master spectrum of **substance** vibrations or "mother wave" —

have countless imprints on it representing countless individual soul patterns.

Let us assume for the sake of discussion that there is soul. Just by ordinary observation, there seems to be more to *self* than just animated body and mind. There seems to be in play a third element, a carrier of information and personality which appears to be more the personality than does the animated body. It is as though the body were a shell through which the personality finds expression. Simple introspection can bring us to this consideration: Since I can look at my body and examine its mechanism in every detail, then **I** must be something apart from my body, however much I may need the body in order to find expression.

The body can hardly be classified as anything more than a complex, highly intricate mechanism of limited durability. Let us say then that *soul* is that third element which carries the personality and peculiar identity of the individual over a long period of time, longer than the limited duration of a physical body. The *soul* is still a part of **substance**, but it is on a frequency band all its own. This particular frequency band of **substance** carries the image of each individual expression. When a physical body takes birth, the two combine to manifest as a conscious entity.

Each personality matches up with a corresponding body, determined by the natural attunement between the two; together they find expression as a *you* or *me*.

Reincarnation, or Oblivion

Into a concept of soul there is also introduced the question of immortality. The soul could certainly be more durable than the body which contains it. It would show differences in development, differences which could not be explained in the period of a single, physical lifetime. One of the most intriguing answers to the question of immortality is the postulation that the soul incarnates with a physical body in a series of lifetimes, continuously building its identity pattern as new experiences add to its overall personality potential.

If reincarnation is the order of soul development, then acceptance of this concept would greatly influence the behavior patterns of society. In the reincarnation theory the effects of one's thoughts and actions do not end with death, but are carried through into another life. One would not look toward death as an end to responsibility, nor look forward to last-minute penitence as an eraser of all that has gone before. This is not to say that the laws of cause and effect are retributive in nature; the laws keep working, and until an effect has taken place or has been mitigated by new actions, the effect will take place according to the causes set into motion.

If people knew this — that they cannot escape the effects of causes set into motion — they would likely take a different stance in life. It wouldn't matter that any misconduct escaped the eyes of the law in this life, for eventually there would be a day of reckoning. Persons could not escape the effects of their behavior, be it good or bad. The inherent structure of BEING strives for balance in all things, and balance will inevitably be effected.

Reincarnation, like anything else, is an assumption based upon an element of logic that is, at the moment, reasonably satisfying. The persons who take the long view of reincarnation are building reserves — reserves of positive thinking, positive actions, positive work in their environment which will not only serve the moment, but will serve them in the distant future when they must, by necessity, again and again be part of that environment.

If reincarnation were accepted by more people, there might possibly be a greater tendency to build for tomorrow. Principles of conservation, health, social management, and personal industry would be of more concern. Tomorrow would be of more concern. Tomorrow would not simply be the concern of some yet unknown generation, but a generation which is largely a regeneration of the present.

In contradistinction to the "judgment-day" concepts in which soul units are sentenced for eternity, a belief in reincarnation is like a breath of spring. No one is *eternally* damned, nor is anyone *eternally* suspended in a hard-to-conceive, non-physical state of exultation and joy. Rather, everyone keeps working out their problems, as it is said, just as they do now. The self learns to appreciate life, for life will be with it for a long time. It learns its lesson well, for it knows that school is never out, and that its progress from one day to the next determines the kind of class and school in which it will be placed as it moves from grade to grade.

Life takes on another hue. People take more time to enjoy the wonders of consciousness. They direct it more toward the beautiful things which life offers. They commune with nature and observe its wonders — taking time to enjoy the sight of a bird, the unfolding of a bud, the movement of cosmic bodies in the sky, the fragrance of things — as vibrations course through their beings. They seek the goodness of people, approach them without fear or rancor, equate them as fellow students treading their various paths in life.

With a belief in reincarnation, people tend to become more serious planners. They relax more, worry less. With more serious planning, their mode of living could change from "eat, drink and be merry, with careless abandon," to "plan, be moderate, proceed carefully and thoughtfully in all that you do."

Life is no less exciting when one takes the long view. It is less disastrous, less lethal, less filled with regrets. The personality with the long view drinks life to the fullest, but not all in one draught. It saves some of its moments of exhilaration and fulfillment for the tomorrow which it knows will surely come.

With belief in reincarnation, there is little tendency for one to look for escapes. There is less of a tendency to run away from problems, because life is essentially a problem-solving affair. In this life and the next, problems linger until they are faced and resolved.

In response to a challenge that personality traits and intelligence are due to heredity rather than to learning in previous incarnations, the concept of reincarnation suggests that heredity and reincarnation go hand in hand. A personality at birth is drawn to and incarnates into a family which provides the conditions and environment equivalent to its development.

A girl might say that her talent for acting is inherited from her mother. It could also be true to say that her talent for acting is carried over from a previous incarnation. The two are interrelated. If a person has a talent for acting, loves acting, and wishes to continue acting in another life, then it would stand to reason that she would be drawn to parents whose physical traits would provide a "hereditary" vehicle for the maximum expression of her talents and experience.

On the negative side, if a man was not particularly ambitious and had no interest in developing himself or in working too hard, he could be attracted to parents of the same demeanor and inclination, for there his quest would be satisfied. It would be incomplete to just flatly state that he is lazy because his parents are lazy. What a person achieves from incarnation to incarnation could be by far the greater determining factor in the talents and potential of the individual. Physical appearances and behaviorisms are, of course, hereditary, but they nevertheless must complement the requirements of the evolving personality, or the two will never mesh and exist as a harmonious entity.

Exacting as reincarnation is in regard to the effects arising out of a person's causative actions, it is not as stringent as some traditional disciplines. The laws of BEING are impersonal in their actions, which allows for a great deal more flexibility in a moral code. To BEING, there is nothing that is intrinsically good or evil. Good and evil are categories of behavior which we have created; basically they are relative to our goals and desires rather than to any universal law. What is good for one may be bad for another, and *vice versa*.

The soul could be considered the basis of *self*. It, like the brain, receives and stores countless impressions which stimulate the consciousness from day to day. It is the unit which carries these impressions as an indelible imprint on its own frequency band.

We should take a moment here to study the particular

relationship between the soul and its consciousness. In order to be conscious of itself, the soul must combine with the frequency configurations in that order of **substance** which makes up our physical or objective reality. *Together* they manifest as a conscious entity. We may think, sometimes, that we can abstract — have mental experiences — without using any part of the body, but this is simply an illusion.

The illustrations we have given up to this point are at best only an effort to describe the indescribable, and there is always the chance that extrasensory messages will be affected or colored by a person's previous experience and mental concepts. This of course is hard to overcome, but we are simply reminding each of you not to judge any of these descriptions and conclusions as hard and fast rules. Surely, continued research with more sophisticated instrumentation and computerized analysis will some day give us more tangible evidence of the vibratory structure of our image world. If there is indeed *soul*, then there may come a day when it can be measured according to its rate of vibration and can be "read" on some electronic device, showing, for example, its personality, character, and depth of information.

EFFICACY OF PRAYER — *Just as we cannot discount such subjects as soul, reincarnation, or precognition, we likewise should look at prayer's place in the omnipresence of God. Simply because God is imminent — however impersonal and ultra-natural — prayer as a process of attunement with the Absolute is as efficacious as prayer ever has been. The idea of seeking help or consolation from the Whole of which we're a part is as relevant within the context of this book as it ever has been. Perhaps one difference might be where you're looking for God and whether you are asking for something outside the Law of BEING.*

DIRECTIONS

*"Inhibition — the control of impulse —
is the first mark of civilization."*
                                                    — Will Durant

Pains of Permissiveness

A word which has made the rounds as a basic cause of human ills is *permissiveness*. Scarcely a civilization in recent history has escaped its affliction. In our times, it has come about partly as a revolt against oppressive social codes which were, in many respects, repressive. The liberals then tried to liberate humanity, to bring more freedom into the lives of individuals and social groups. They won many adherents and today, for all practical purposes, we can say that they are carrying the ball. Like any good ball team, they are committed to going all the way. Instead of achieving just a simple balance, which is the ideal social state, they are carrying society into another state of imbalance. If they go unchecked we will experience an upheaval, the severity of which would be determined by the degree of imbalance reached.

In order to escape the ill effects of unbridled permissiveness, some braking effect must be placed on the present trend of the liberation movement. The monumental question is: Where and how much? The answer is not simple and requires more than just words. To hold the line against a runaway situation requires massive teamwork by a sizable portion of humanity. Here we must clearly define our goals so that we do not simply crush the opposition and create another runaway situation in the opposite direction.

The goal for a happy, well-adjusted society is *moderation*. Since we are part of a universal system in which **force** acts in opposing directions, we will always be faced with the situation of these two directions vying for advantage. "The pendulum swings" — so says an ancient writing. Opposition and differences are inevitable; they are ever-present factors of life.

Moderation and balance are not natural states. They are conditions which man must initiate and maintain if he is to experience peace of mind and harmony. Many have a tendency to think of nature as one harmonious whole, believing that to achieve happiness, all we have to do is go back to nature. This philosophy is quite prevalent today, but Nature is constantly on the move, and in its eternal motion it is often moving toward a state of imbalance. In nature, balance often is only achieved by upheaval, by the superior attraction of one element forcing another element into its sphere. Then for a time there is balance, but in the next instant of time, elements are pulling or pushing against each other, insisting on change and disruption.

Mind is an attribute of BEING which can bring order out of chaos. People, who undoubtedly express the largest share of **mind** on Earth, have not utilized their full potential by a long way. Yet the potential is there for us to use; with our minds in full gear, we can, to a large extent, avoid or modify the disruptions of our natural state. Instead of just sitting around waiting for things to happen, we can check the full onslaught of the happening, altering its course or dividing it into bits and pieces which we can handle. Instead of waiting for Nature to build up great pressures which could explode with cataclysmic **force**, we can discharge these pressures little by little so that there is an even flow. In this way we can achieve moderation.

Let us cite some examples. A running stream flowing to the sea is an uncontrolled, natural phenomenon. The stream flows in a state of uninhibited liberation, free to go where it chooses, unmindful of the potential for harm and destruction it carries in its wake. As a free agent, it causes floods on the one hand and droughts on the other. On its own, it achieves no balance between the two.

We can — and do — control this phenomenon in many instances. We build dams with spillways so that the flow of water becomes steady and predictable. The dam with the spillway is an example of moderation. A dam without a spillway is an example of repression; it would result in an upheaval similar to the ones which occurred when the water ran free.

In our use of electrical and nuclear energy, we use similar methods to bring about a controlled state of equilibrium. These energies are repressed, then liberated, in calculated degrees so that the cycle of pent-up pressures and cataclysmically released pressures is broken.

In order to achieve equilibrium in human affairs, the same rules apply. If moderation means controlled release of forces and pressures in nature, then that's what it means in human affairs. This is not the easiest path for people to take, however, even though it is the most fulfilling and harmonious path.

It takes mature minds to undertake controlled release of pressures in human relationships. The mature mind is not humanity's long suit yet, but it is our hope for the future. Then we will achieve equilibrium through controlled use of permissive and repressive behavior. We will build safety valves into our social codes so that the great pressures will no longer build up. We can harness human behavior just as proficiently and advantageously as we have harnessed other natural forces. Instead of taking our chances with nature, we will direct the course of our lives by properly channeling human emotions. We will give and take in calculated proportions, being neither afraid to say, "No," when we feel we are right, or, "Yes," when we feel that another is right.

Moderation means keeping people informed. Don't keep others in the dark. *Ignorance builds pressure.* Through our extensive capacity for communications today, we have the wherewithal to achieve an enlightened community.

Moderation means sharing, apportioning the fruits of our labors to those who shared in that labor and giving *equitable* distribution of wealth to all participants. *Selfishness builds up pressure.*

Moderation means consideration of others — not forcing one upon the other, but allowing both to live with equal opportunity. *Prejudice builds up pressures.*

Moderation means equanimity, not exploding in anger — the most disastrous of emotional outbursts. While it often quickly relieves the angry person, its fallout on others burns long and deep. *Rage builds up pressure.*

Moderation means tolerance. This is not to say that wrongs should be excused, but neither should there be excessive or meaningless punishment for wrongdoers. *Injustice builds up pressure.*

To determine *where* and *how much* braking to do on today's trend toward an overly permissive society, the *where* is in every avenue of our lives. All must put brakes on their own involvement with others wherever they see permissive behavior getting out of hand. For *how much,* each person must brake to the extent that a happy medium is reached.

If we are to "save the world," the answer is not in scurrying around looking for more energy, more food or more land, in order to accommodate a population explosion. The answer is in curbing population growth. Even conservation cannot forestall the cataclysmic effects of a regular doubling of population on a planet already in danger of depleting its life support system.

Education – Bulwark of An Enlightened Society

It is in the early years of a person's life that guidance programs have the greatest significance. It is then that character and body building come easiest. It is then that we should make every effort to see that a good start is made available to every child. This is no more a family's responsibility than it is society's.

In any group, the health and welfare of each member is vitally important to the health and welfare of the group, and by now everyone should have realized that if there are troublemakers in the group, no member of the group is assured of *imperturbability*.

In building character in those early years, there should be no choice on a child's part as to whether or not he wants to do the right thing. In many instances, you may have heard a parent admonish a child, "I don't want you to go outside in the cold without a coat. If you do, don't come running to me when your nose starts running, expecting to get out of going to school."

In another instance, you may have heard a parent warn a child not to touch things as they walk through a toy store, for if he or she does, it might spoil the merchandise for someone else — or if it is damaged, he or she will have to pay for it.

Once you make an admonishment, you are expressing your will on what you want done. After that it is up to you to see that it *is* done. Otherwise, do not make the admonishment. If it is not done, then you have a responsibility to correct the behavior by some sort of example. By doing this for the first four or five years, you can rest more securely when the child begins to do things outside the family environment.

These are cautions teachers might follow as well. If you are teaching children to spell, and some have more difficulty than others, it is too simplistic to just write them off with a low grade. They are there to learn to spell, and they should come out of that class knowing how to spell, no matter how much extra time is needed to do this. The same can be said for most other subjects. There's no real excuse for their not performing on these early basics, especially when there is a fundamental consensus in society that everyone should be able to read, write, spell, and know elementary arithmetic.

From the very beginning, children should be trained to think and work in harmony with nature's requirements. They should be trained to adjust to the change and motion of BEING, to the pushing and pulling of the **force** around them, to the behavior patterns which electromagnetism brings. They should be helped and disciplined to forestall procrastination and indolence by activity programs which will fill their bodies and minds with constructive and harmonious components.

Society as a whole should take an active part in the total life program of its children. Schools which are fully integrated with the home and community can offer study, work and recreational activities beyond the present school hours, acting in a manner which will eliminate the sad plight of children who have nothing to do and nowhere to go because of a lack of interest or direction outside of school.

In such a program, the children would assume part of the care and responsibility of community life. Education would not be simply a matter of going to school so many hours a day, but also a practice in the art of living. The entire community would share in the school program and would gain not only from the services rendered by the children, but also from the overall good effect of a completely well-informed, participating society.

This would fill the gap left by society's move from rural to urban areas. Rural areas, for the most part, provide a fountain of activity for the young — a series of chores at home, before and after school hours. Countless parents now mourn the loss of that aspect of "the good old days." Instead of mourning, however, they should accept the challenge of finding ways to fill the gap in an age when technology takes on so many of the "chores" of yesterday. And, of course, it can be done!

In the formative years, great stress should be placed on basic drills in reading, 'riting and 'rithmetic. Following these "must" skills, expression exercises should rank high in importance. This would involve creative activities from acting to painting, from gardening to cleaning. In older age groups, the forms of expression would become more sophisticated, but with a continuing emphasis on expression, communication skills, and knowing the world.

Well-adjusted individuals should be able to express themselves, to make themselves heard. Without these most essential tools of communication, they would soon find themselves at a disadvantage in society, with a resulting sense of insecurity. To further overcome this, each child's special gift should be sought out and developed so that *everyone is good at something.*

Of equal importance to these mental development techniques is a basic physical fitness program. Good health is very important to a well-adjusted life, and physical fitness should have as much attention as mental fitness. This would involve lessons in hygiene, diet and physiology, with a solid schedule of calisthenics. Competitive games of all sorts would fill every person with a sense of belonging and achieving.

Another area of the curriculum which warrants greater attention is the pace at which children learn and assimilate. More continuity in every area of education might be advantageous. Rather than scurrying from room to room and subject to subject at the sound of a bell, more time in a given subject area and more time for adjustment from one area to another might lead to better assimilation of subjects and more integration between teacher and student.

With a more leisurely pace during school hours, with subjects which are meaningful and useful, with a continuation of the learning process in off-school hours, children should experience a happier and healthier attitude toward their growth years.

An expanded program such as this would provide its own monitors and teachers, as older children begin to assume those responsibilities as part of their curriculum. All of this needs a great deal of planning and commitment on the part of society, but it is something which bears considerable thought and consensus. Its value to society is immeasurable.

The Moral Equation

Morality is mostly a human concern. It is a sense of knowing what is right or wrong in the course of events. It is the cornerstone of human society. It speaks of a behavior relationship between the self and the environment. When this kind of relationship breaks down, we face a moral crisis. The result is that such values as selflessness, sharing, honesty, integrity, ethics, respect and fair play are put aside, and self-interest becomes a damaging plague which threatens society's very existence.

Historically, the guidelines for morality have been set down in the words and writings of philosophers in our past, usually emphasizing the same theme — behavior which is good and behavior which is bad. Goodness triumphing over evil is the essence of their theme, and that theme has not changed with time.

Few people would dispute the notion that goodness is better than evil, but we have fallen short in our attempt to *demonstrate* that good is better than evil — that goodness will indeed be rewarded and evil will be repaid in kind. In our experience, we often perceive the "bad" going unpunished and the "good" going unrewarded.

One reason for this apparent disparity is that neither good nor bad is easy to define. Although there are some generally loose agreements — in a very broad sense — on what is bad and what is good, there are almost as many definitions of the two as there are people.

There is a second reason why society has failed to *demonstrate* that good will earn good in return and that bad will earn bad: society has made little effort to gather empirical evidence on the subject of morality. For the most part, the subject has been kept out of the mainstream of public educational programs and left to religious-philosophical approaches; all too often, these approaches are anything but empirical. Their commitment to after-death states of existence — wherein final rewards and punishment are meted out — is an answer which no longer satisfies a growing number of people.

To these people, belief and faith are not sufficient to answer society's most pressing questions on moral behavior.

So, as a society, there is, by and large, a lot of guessing on the whole issue of morality. We may have only the faintest idea of what's going on "out there" in the enormity of the universe, of what's expected of us in the way of behavior, of what will be the results of our behavior, bad or good.

Moral behavior depends on knowing for sure *what* is right and *what* is wrong. By not knowing, by having no clear-cut guidelines, there is certainly cause for frustration and wrongdoing — for going ahead with almost careless abandon on a course which follows the line of least resistance. Such a course, as we have seen, is a primary cause behind "wrong behavior."

Moral behavior also depends on a set of believable and reasonable rules and an enforcement agency to curb the tendency to break the rules. Without such an agency, rules and codes soon lose their effectiveness. However, rules should be few, simply stated and relevant. When people are mired down by a mountain of rules — few of which they can even remember, many of which are never enforced, few of which are relevant to everyone alike — is it any wonder that rules are broken and forgotten?

If there is anything in life to which people everywhere are sensitive, it is **fair play**. It is not always the rightness or wrongness of an incident which plagues our sensibilities as much as it is the degree and kind of discipline invoked on all parties in a given incident.

Enforcement can take many forms, such as civil laws, parental disciplines, and the building of habit patterns which become self-enforcers. Whatever form it takes, it is essential that the rules to be enforced apply to everyone alike and that the penalties for breaking rules are just as fairly prescribed.

Penalties should be designed to teach a lesson. They should be severe enough so that the very thought of them is repulsive. However, long-term confinements, fines, death, or hell-fire are, generally speaking, not particularly effective deterrents.

Leading a moral life, in which everything we do is right, is essentially a matter of living in harmony with our environment, and for that we need to have a clear understanding of the environment — *"to know where we are, and whither we are tending."*

We need to know with what we're harmonizing. It isn't enough to say, "with nature." It isn't enough to say, "with God." Who or what is Nature? Who or what is God? What do we mean by harmonizing? What is there about us — and them — that necessitates our working for harmony? We don't have strings like a violin, nor valves like a flute. And we certainly don't have much of an idea about with what in Nature or God we're supposed to harmonize. Is it the weather, the shape of the earth, the heavenly bodies? Is it the vastness of the universe, its power, its sense of BEING?

One thing is certain: the harmonizing process begins with us. Though the variations within the process are many, we have two basic options. One is to get in step with Nature; the other is to have Nature get in step with us. We spend a great deal of time in trying to get others to see things our way — often a fruitless pursuit— and a great deal less time trying to see things their way. In society, compromise is the order of the day!

This is perfectly normal behavior, of course, and in the preceding pages, our main point of reference was the delicate balance which exists between what we want and what the environment can, or will, provide. Balance is our constant goal, and when we achieve it, we are for that moment at peace with the world.

These moments aren't always the most difficult part to achieve, however, because the opportunities are ever present; there are few people who do not have "their moments," however fleeting.

Your greatest ally in coping with the phenomenon of Nature is a knowledge of its components and requirements. One of the many steps toward achieving a more lasting balance is to welcome the process, looking at change not only as a necessary fact of life, but also as a break in the humdrum which might be your existence.

Summing Up

All of the foregoing indicate a strong sense of options for the individual: a freedom to go with or against the tide, to adjust or not adjust, to procrastinate or not procrastinate, to love or not love, to explore or not explore. There is very little you actually *must* do to maintain a *status quo*. But lest you develop an attitude that just because you are more free to do as you please, you will do less, let us point out that simply because you aren't required to do something is no reason for not doing it. Being *free* only means that you have a *greater responsibility* to see that you do the things which are best for you.

> *The freedom you gain in a more democratic society is not a freedom from responsibility, but only a freedom to take on more responsibility yourself, rather than passing it on to others.*

We are in a state of transition, and the burst of freedom so many people enjoy today causes them to romp and play almost with careless abandon. It's just so good to be free! But people will settle down. They will find that they must impose their own restrictions and disciplines for health and happiness. The more we can do to emphasize this need, the more quickly will society again straighten itself out.

People should experience the optimum sense of freedom in every way: freedom to think what they will; freedom to act out their own destiny; freedom to choose their friends, place of abode, means of employment; freedom to move about and experience the fullness of life. This is the goal of a free society — to give its members the fullest quotient of freedom possible, both mentally and physically.

Part and parcel of this ideal, however, is to educate the people to such a responsibility so that they can handle freedom when they have it.

You cannot offer people quick methods of physical or mental development, hoping to have them prepared to handle this growth without considerable guidance and education along the way. The practice of attempting to free people from their inhibitions in just a few counseling sessions is especially hazardous. The releasing of inhibitions or memory patterns from one's past is a kind of freedom, but it needs to be cultivated slowly and carefully — not left "just hanging there" without redirection and substitution.

From countless persons there are laments on the failures of our age. They seem to see at every turn manifestations of violence, dishonesty, anarchy, lasciviousness, indolence, and unbridled selfishness. There are also those who are generally complacent, averse to change, trying to hold on to the "good old days," or afraid to meet the challenges of a dynamic society. They are basically insecure, not sure enough of themselves to withstand criticism or interruption of their beliefs and practices. They not only fear violence and rebellion, they also fear *any* change in the status quo.

Dark as they may paint the picture of society today, the trend of the times is not regression, but a positive progression toward new standards of conduct. Society today is less afraid to question its past, its traditions, its time-honored beliefs. It is less afraid of honesty and frankness in its interaction with itself.

In the "good old days" people were crueler to people, crueler to animals, crueler to even the land and its resources. People were cruel because they were ignorant. Ignorance breeds superstition and fear, and in fear people can be very cruel. They strike out at the unknown — at that which might hurt them and at that which someone tells them might hurt them. In ignorance they are easily led, led by those who use their knowledge to rule and gain advantage over others.

As society becomes more educated, more knowing about this environment, it becomes less fearful and consequently less cruel. It becomes sophisticated, mature, able to handle itself in any situation.

Communication is the key to today's growing awareness. People are talking and listening to each other; they are inquiring, learning, and discussing any subject without the prejudice and fear of reprisal which is so often a barrier to their best intentions.

We must expect that when people are free to learn, free to experiment, free to explore, they will investigate many things and experiment with many things, both positive and negative. The important thing is that people are in a learning mode these days. They have communication with the "world outside," and will ultimately be in a position to choose that which is most harmonious. This is the best guarantee society can have that all people will someday enjoy the fact of being alive on this planet.

With the image of God as we have defined it in this text, many persons may be asking themselves: "Where do we go from here?" What of our cherished beliefs and notions? If we begin questioning them and considering new concepts as outlined in this text, how do we interface with those about us who cling to the "tried and true" past?

This is not a panic situation. A person's beliefs do not change the *actuality* of BEING. Life can go on as it is without there being any change in the true state of existence. New ideas, like seeds, need time to incubate and develop in a person's consciousness. The more prepared people are — by virtue of their previous readings, experience, and existing philosophies — the easier it will be to assimilate this matter.

Our eternal quest is *imperturbability*; this is already achievable in part, or in whole, by almost everyone, regardless of any person's level of consciousness.

If the story of Santa Claus brings a sense of happiness and imperturbability to our children, for example, and a lesson of giving and loving and sharing as well, how can we fault that? Children grow out of the story, but they flourish as they begin to question the "magic" in the Santa myth, without losing the lesson.

And so it is with the myths and legends of our

adulthood. There is no reason to sever our participation in those that serve us in the sense of bringing *imperturbability*.

However we define God in the absolute sense, and however impersonal and formless God may be in the absolute sense, we should not lose sight of the fact that the compassion, love, and form which manifest in our *reality* are attributes of God as well. All of our various representations of the *actuality* of God, serve to give us focal points to which we can address our yearnings for inspiration and guidance.

Ritualization is part of our total life experience in which the **substance**, **force** and **mind** of BEING take form. The images and behaviorisms which we assign to God in our *reality* are parts of a story form which we commonly use to relate the great principles of Nature to the experiences of our daily lives.

Those who fear that the freedom of thought and expression will lead to anarchy —a historic concern of society — should be reminded that the forces to control and moderate such a threat will be equally forthcoming.

We end with a final quotation:

> *"Enlighten the populace generally, and*
> *tyranny and oppressions of body and mind*
> *will vanish like evil spirits at the dawn of day."*
>
> — Thomas Jefferson

INDEX

Additional copies of
IN THE IMAGE OF GOD
by Arthur C. Piepenbrink

may be ordered
by sending a check or money order
for $12.95 postpaid for each copy to:

DISTINCTIVE PUBLISHING CORP.
P.O. Box 17868
Plantation, FL 33318-7868
(305) 975-2413

Quantity discounts are also available
from the publisher